Collins Primary Atlas

Contents

D1423769

Globes

Globes are models of the earth. They show the true shape and size of the continents.

North America lies between the Atlantic and Pacific Oceans.

South America is mostly in the southern hemisphere and extends south towards Antarctica.

Europe is one of the smallest continents.

Antarctica encircles the South Pole.

Oceania is made up of Australia, New Zealand and many small islands.

Asia is the largest continent.

Africa is almost equally balanced either side of the equator.

Map projections

To show the world on a flat map we need to peel the surface of the globe and flatten it out. There are many different methods of altering the shape of the earth so that it can be mapped on an atlas page. These methods are called **projections**.

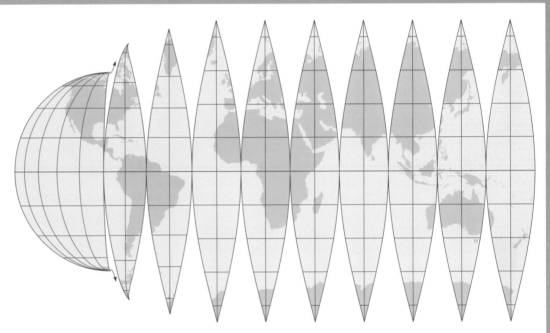

This is how the earth would look if the surface could be peeled and laid flat.

Map projections change the shape and size of the continents and oceans. The projection used for world maps in this atlas is called Eckert IV.

How the world map looks, depends on which continents are at the centre of the map. Compare the shape of Africa on the maps below to that on the globe.

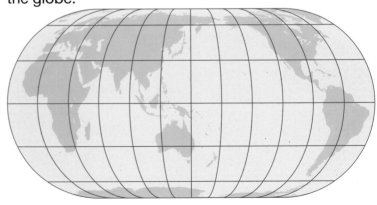

For UK atlases the world would look like this.

For Australian atlases the world would look like this.

We use latitude and longitude to locate places on the earth's surface. Lines of **latitude** are imaginary lines. They are numbered in degrees North or South of the equator.

Lines of **longitude** are imaginary lines which run from the North to the South Poles. They are numbered in degrees East or West of a line through London known as the Greenwich Meridian.

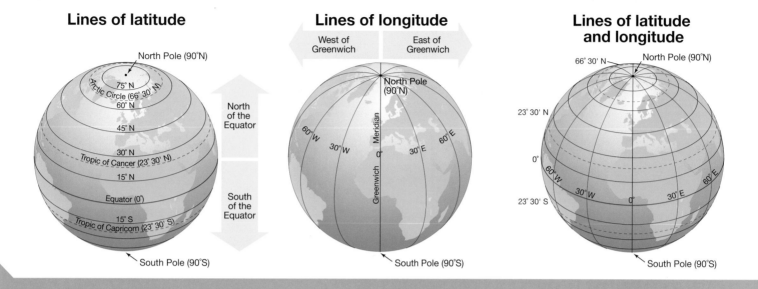

Hemispheres

The equator divides the globe into two halves. All land north of the equator is called the northern hemisphere. Land south of the equator is called the southern hemisphere. 0° and 180° lines of longitude also divide the globes into two imaginary halves, the western and eastern hemispheres.

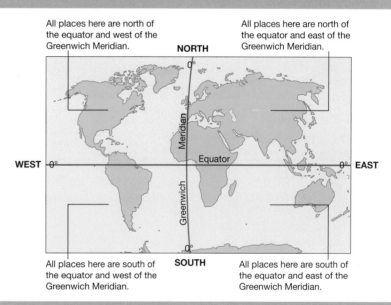

Grid references

As well as using lines of latitude to find places, this atlas uses grids. The columns are labelled with a letter and the rows with a number. The grid code (e.g. B6) can be used to find all places within one grid square.

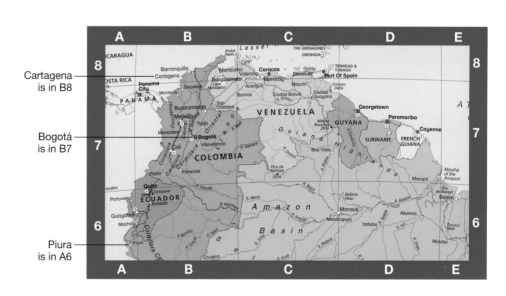

Atlas maps help us to find out what places are like.
They tell us about different environments in the world.

Some maps show country shapes and where towns are located within the country. These are called political maps.

Some maps show landscapes. They show the physical environment.

Understanding maps

Special names and numbers are used to label parts of an atlas map.

Page number
This helps you to find out where the map you want is in the atlas.

Locator map
This shows the part of the world covered by the map.

Key
This explains what the colours and symbols used on the map represent.

Scale
This explains how large a map is. It helps to work out distances between places. See page 6 to find out more about scale.

Title
This names the map area and describes what the map shows.

Compass
This always points north-south on the map. It shows east and west. Other directions can be found from the compass.

Fact boxes
These contain interesting information about a continent.

Area comparison
This map shows the size of the British Isles compared to the region mapped.

The statue known as Christ the Redeemer overlooks Rio de Janeiro.

The ruins of the lost Inca city of Machu Picchu in Peru.

Scale : One centimetre on this map is the same as 400 kilometres on the ground.

Map symbols

Maps are made up of symbols and names. The symbols can be points, lines or area colours.
A map is complete when the symbols and the names are combined.

Point symbols

- ■○ Town stamps
- ▲ Mountain peaks
- ✈ Airports

Lines

- —— Roads
- ┅┅ Railways
- —— Rivers
- —— Coastline

Area colours

- ▢ Lake/sea
- ◤ Country colours

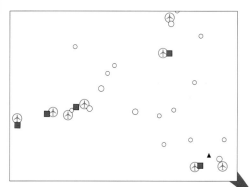

Point symbols are used on a map to show towns, mountain peaks and airports.

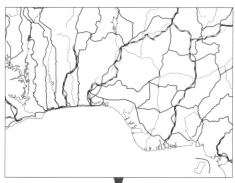

Lines are used on a map to show communications and drainage.

Area colours are used to distinguish one country from another and the land from the sea.

Names on atlas maps

The style and size of the type used on maps helps to explain what the name means.

Large bodies of water

PACIFIC OCEAN

Gulf of Guinea

Islands

Cuba

Bioco

Countries

N I G E R I A

BENIN

Large cities

Porto-Novo

Lomé

Small towns

Parakou

Enugu

Rivers

R. Mississippi

R. Nile

R. Amazon

Mountain peaks

Mount Cameroon

Mount Everest

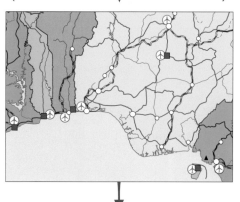

All the symbols are combined to show features and their correct locations.

Names are needed to show places and features shown on the map. Only some places and features are named.

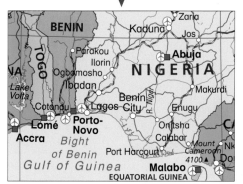

The map is complete when the symbols and the names are combined.

Scale

Maps are much smaller than the regions they show. To compare the real area with the mapped area you have to use a scale. Each map in this atlas shows its scale. This is shown using a scale bar which is explained in words.

E.g.
0   200   400   600   800 km

Scale : One centimetre on this map is the same as 200 kilometres on the ground.

Large scale

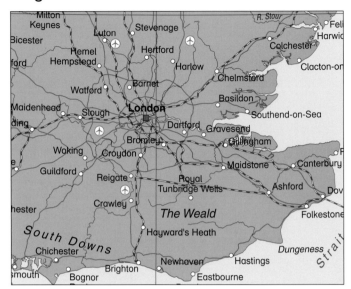

Scale : One centimetre on this map is the same as 20 kilometres on the ground.

0   20   40   60   80   100 km

Large scale maps show smaller areas with more detail.

Measuring distance

The scale of a map can be used to measure how far it is between two places. For example, the straight line distance between Boa Vista and Cayenne on the map to the right is 5 centimetres.

Look at the ruler.
One centimetre on this map is the same as 200 kilometres on the ground. The real distance between Boa Vista and Cayenne is therefore 1000 kilometres (i.e. 5 x 200).

0   200   400   600   800 km   Scale : One centimetre on

Medium scale

Scale : One centimetre on this map is the same as 250 kilometres on the ground.

0   250   500   750   1000   1250 km

Small scale

Scale : One centimetre on this map is the same as 800 kilometres on the ground.

0   800   1600   2400   3200 km

Small scale maps show larger areas with less detail.

p is the same as 200 kilometres on the ground.

Finding directions

Directions help you to work out which way to go when you travel from place to place. There are four main compass directions: North (N), East (E), South (S) and West (W). These are called the cardinal points. The compass can also be divided in eight points as shown in the diagram below.

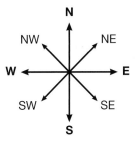

An eight-point compass

The needle of the compass always points to the north because it is magnetic. Maps are usually drawn to match the compass with north at the top and south at the bottom.

The Solar System

The Solar System is the Sun and the many objects that orbit it. These objects include eight planets, at least five dwarf planets and countless asteroids, meteoroids and comets. Orbiting some of the planets and dwarf planets are over 160 moons. The Sun keeps its surrounding objects in its orbit by its pull of gravity which has an influence for many millions of kilometres.

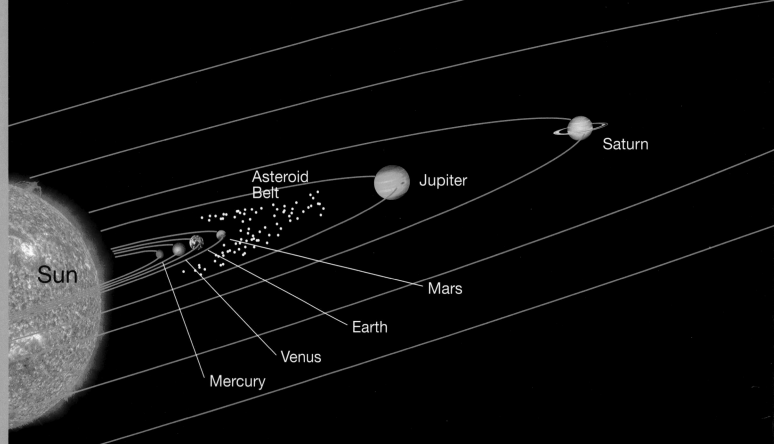

Saturn

Jupiter

Asteroid Belt

Mars

Earth

Venus

Mercury

Sun

Planets of the Inner Solar System

PLANET $\longrightarrow$	Mercury	Venus	Earth	Mars
DISTANCE $\longrightarrow$ (from the Sun)	58 million kilometres	108 million kilometres	150 million kilometres	228 million kilometres

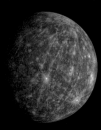

Mercury is the smallest planet and closest to the Sun.

Venus lies between Earth and the Sun. It is the brightest object in the sky.

Earth is the only planet in the Universe known to support life. Most of its surface is covered in water.

Mars is known as the red planet. It has a mountain which rises 24 kilometres above the land.

Neptune

Uranus

Sun

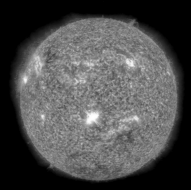

The Sun is a huge ball of hot glowing gases. Heat and light from the Sun travel millions of kilometres to reach Earth and support all life on our planet.

Planets of the Outer Solar System

Jupiter	Saturn	Uranus	Neptune	← PLANET
778 million kilometres	1427 million kilometres	2871 million kilometres	4498 million kilometres	← DISTANCE (from the Sun)

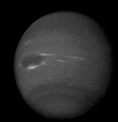

Jupiter is one of the giant planets. It is more than 300 times bigger than Earth.

Saturn is often called the 'ringed planet' because it is surrounded by rings of dust and rocks.

Uranus is known as the 'blue planet'. It orbits the Sun on its side.

Neptune lies furthest from the Sun, and is the windiest planet in the Solar System.

Only one side of the Moon is visible from Earth, the far side has only been seen by the few astronauts whose spaceships orbited it in the late 1960s and early 1970s.

Earth and its Moon compared

Plato

Mare
Imbrium
(Sea of Rains)

Montes Apeninus

Mare
Serenitatis
(Sea of Serenity)

Oceanus
Procellarum
(Ocean of Storms)

Copernicus

Mare
Tranquillitatis
(Sea of Tranquility)

*Apollo 11 landing site
(first men on the moon)*

Mare
Nubium
(Sea of Clouds)

Tycho

The phases of the Moon

| New moon | Waxing crescent | First quarter | Waxing gibbous | Full moon | Waning gibbous | Last quarter | Waning crescent | New moon |

The new moon is not visible from Earth

The Earth's axis is tilted from perpendicular therefore different parts of the globe are oriented towards the Sun at different times of the year. The four seasons, Spring, Summer, Autumn and Winter are a result of this.

December 21

The Sun is overhead at the Tropic of Capricorn. The North Pole is inclined away from the Sun and is in total darkness. The Northern Hemisphere experiences Winter for three months while the Southern Hemisphere experiences Summer.

March 21

The Sun is overhead at the Equator and both the North and South poles are equidistant from the Sun. The Northern Hemisphere experiences Spring for three months while the Southern Hemisphere experiences Autumn.

Sun

June 21

The Sun is overhead at the Tropic of Cancer. The North Pole is inclined towards the Sun and has 24 hour daylight. The Northern Hemisphere experiences Summer for three months while the Southern Hemisphere experiences Winter.

September 21

The Sun is overhead at the Equator and both the North and South poles are equidistant from the Sun. The Northern Hemisphere experiences Autumn for three months while the Southern Hemisphere experiences Spring.

Day and night

The Earth rotates on its axis every 24 hours. At any moment in time one side of the Earth is in sunlight, while the other half is in darkness.

Direction of rotation

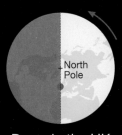

Dawn in the UK

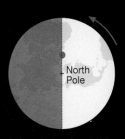

Midday in the UK

Dusk in the UK

Midnight in the UK

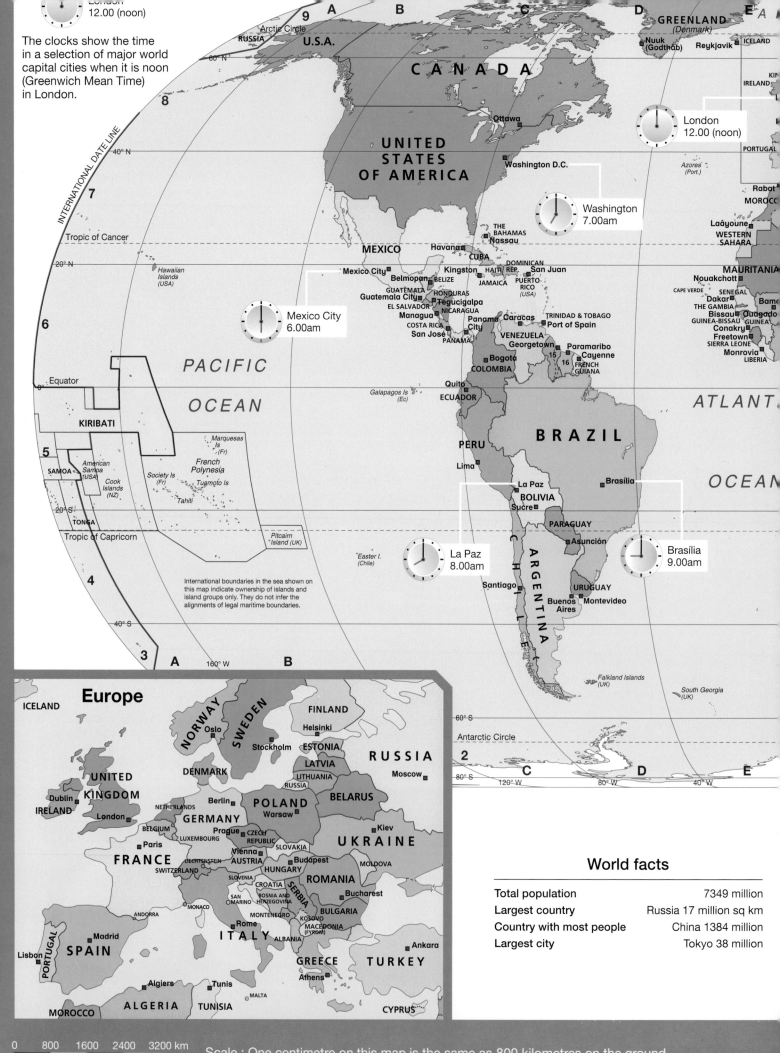

London
12.00 (noon)

The clocks show the time in a selection of major world capital cities when it is noon (Greenwich Mean Time) in London.

London
12.00 (noon)

Washington
7.00am

Mexico City
6.00am

La Paz
8.00am

Brasília
9.00am

Europe

World facts

Total population	7349 million
Largest country	Russia 17 million sq km
Country with most people	China 1384 million
Largest city	Tokyo 38 million

International boundaries in the sea shown on this map indicate ownership of islands and island groups only. They do not infer the alignments of legal maritime boundaries.

Scale : One centimetre on this map is the same as 800 kilometres on the ground.

0 800 1600 2400 3200 km

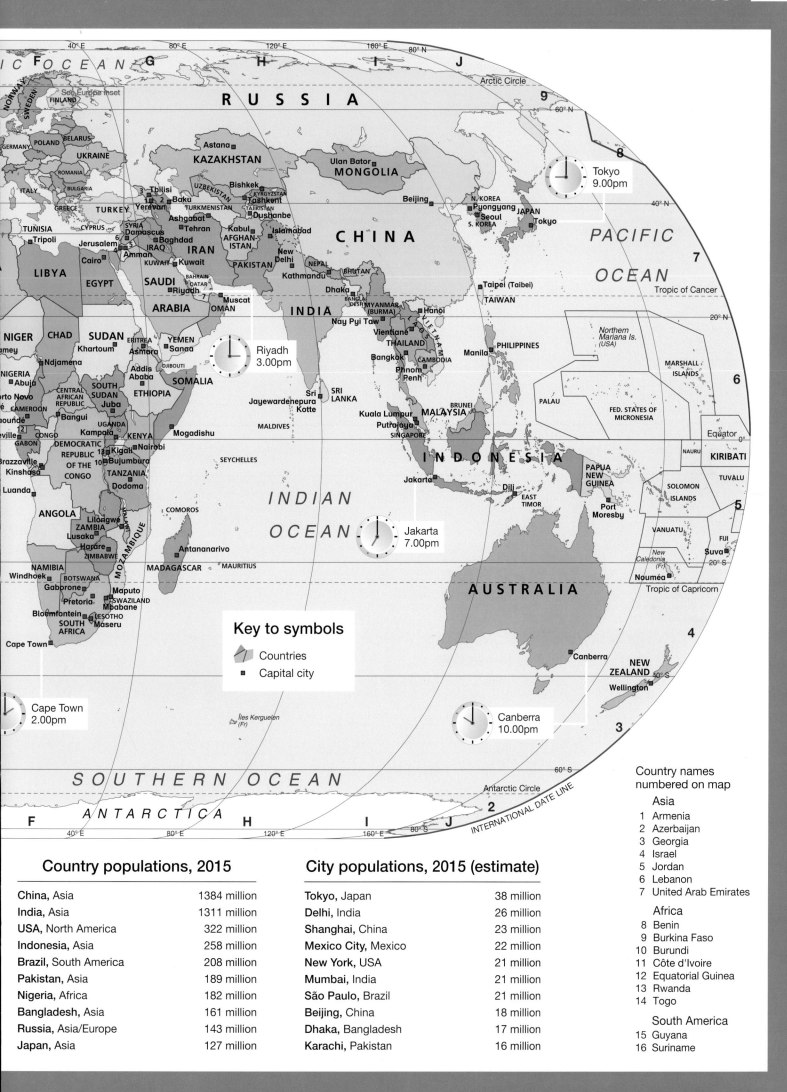

Key to symbols

- Countries
- Capital city

Tokyo 9.00pm

Riyadh 3.00pm

Jakarta 7.00pm

Canberra 10.00pm

Cape Town 2.00pm

Country populations, 2015

Country	Population
China, Asia	1384 million
India, Asia	1311 million
USA, North America	322 million
Indonesia, Asia	258 million
Brazil, South America	208 million
Pakistan, Asia	189 million
Nigeria, Africa	182 million
Bangladesh, Asia	161 million
Russia, Asia/Europe	143 million
Japan, Asia	127 million

City populations, 2015 (estimate)

Tokyo, Japan	38 million
Delhi, India	26 million
Shanghai, China	23 million
Mexico City, Mexico	22 million
New York, USA	21 million
Mumbai, India	21 million
São Paulo, Brazil	21 million
Beijing, China	18 million
Dhaka, Bangladesh	17 million
Karachi, Pakistan	16 million

Country names numbered on map

Asia
1 Armenia
2 Azerbaijan
3 Georgia
4 Israel
5 Jordan
6 Lebanon
7 United Arab Emirates

Africa
8 Benin
9 Burkina Faso
10 Burundi
11 Côte d'Ivoire
12 Equatorial Guinea
13 Rwanda
14 Togo

South America
15 Guyana
16 Suriname

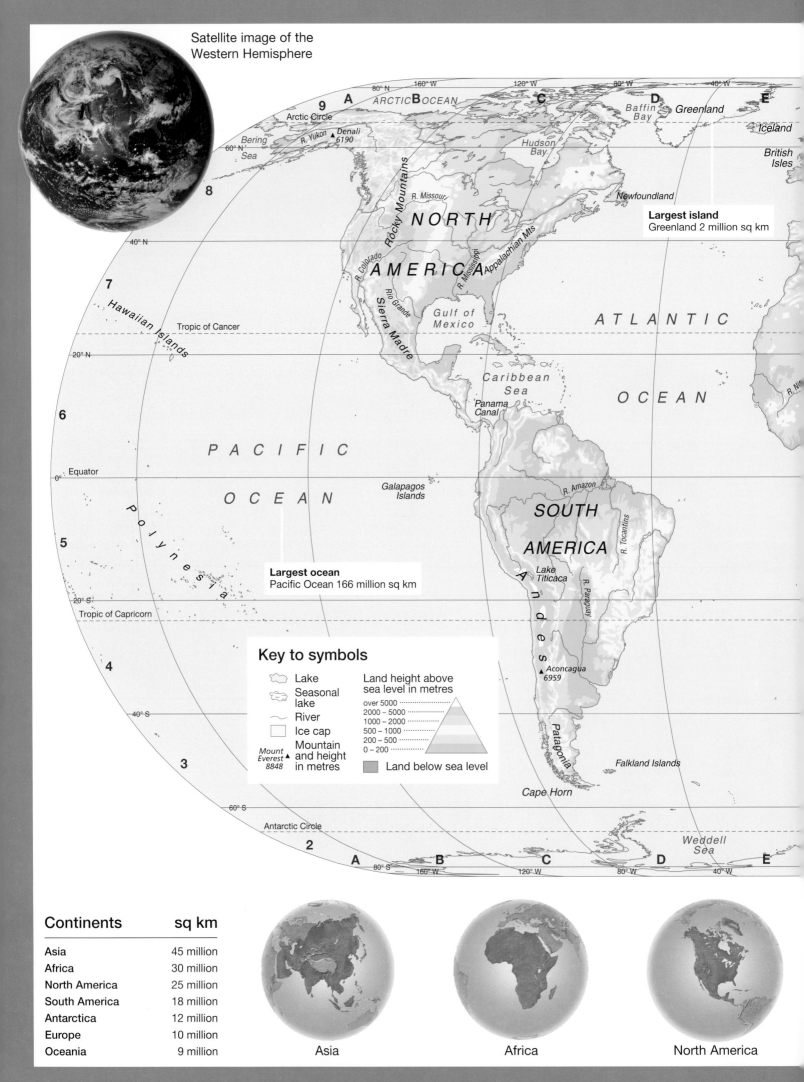

Satellite image of the Western Hemisphere

ARCTIC OCEAN

Arctic Circle

Bering Sea

R. Yukon ▲ Denali 6190

Baffin Bay

Greenland

Iceland

British Isles

Hudson Bay

Newfoundland

Largest island
Greenland 2 million sq km

Rocky Mountains

NORTH

R. Missouri

AMERICA

R. Colorado

R. Mississippi

Appalachian Mts

ATLANTIC

Sierra Madre

Rio Grande

Gulf of Mexico

Tropic of Cancer

Hawaiian Islands

OCEAN

R. Nil

Caribbean Sea

Panama Canal

PACIFIC

Galapagos Islands

R. Amazon

OCEAN

SOUTH

R. Tocantins

AMERICA

Polynesia

Largest ocean
Pacific Ocean 166 million sq km

Andes

Lake Titicaca

R. Paraguay

Tropic of Capricorn

Aconcagua 6959

Key to symbols

⬡ Lake

🝙 Seasonal lake

〜 River

⬜ Ice cap

Mount Everest ▲ 8848 Mountain and height in metres

Land height above sea level in metres

over 5000
2000 – 5000
1000 – 2000
500 – 1000
200 – 500
0 – 200

⬜ Land below sea level

Patagonia

Falkland Islands

Cape Horn

Antarctic Circle

Weddell Sea

Continents

Continents	sq km
Asia	45 million
Africa	30 million
North America	25 million
South America	18 million
Antarctica	12 million
Europe	10 million
Oceania	9 million

Asia

Africa

North America

0 800 1600 2400 3200 km

Scale : One centimetre on this map is the same as 800 kilometres on the ground.

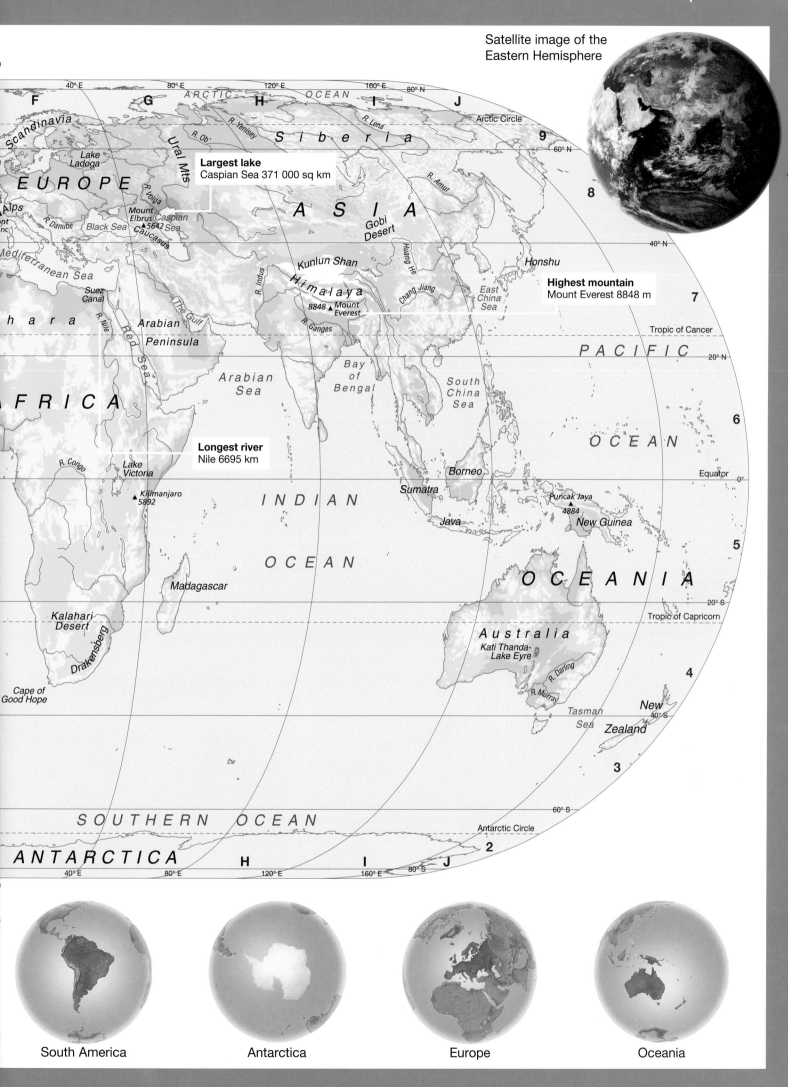

Satellite image of the
Eastern Hemisphere

Largest lake
Caspian Sea 371 000 sq km

Highest mountain
Mount Everest 8848 m

Longest river
Nile 6695 km

F G H I J

40° E   80° E   120° E   160° E   80° N

ARCTIC OCEAN

R. Ob'   R. Yenisey   R. Lena   Arctic Circle   9

Scandinavia   S i b e r i a   60° N

Lake
Ladoga   Ural Mts   8

EUROPE   A S I A   R. Amur

Mount
Elbrus Caspian
▲5642 Sea   Gobi
Desert   Honshu   40° N

Alps   R. Volga   Caspian
Sea   Huang He

R. Danube   Black Sea   Caucasus   Kunlun Shan   East
China
Sea   7

Mediterranean Sea   H i m a l a y a   Chang Jiang

Suez
Canal   8848 ▲ Mount
Everest   Tropic of Cancer

hara   R. Nile   The Gulf   Arabian
Peninsula   R. Indus   R. Ganges   P A C I F I C   20° N

Arabian
Sea   Bay
of
Bengal   South
China
Sea   6

AFRICA   O C E A N

R. Congo   Lake
Victoria   Borneo   Equator   0°

Sumatra   Puncak Jaya
▲
4884

▲ Kilimanjaro
5892   I N D I A N   Java   New Guinea   5

O C E A N   O C E A N I A

Madagascar   20° S

Kalahari
Desert   Tropic of Capricorn

Drakensberg   A u s t r a l i a

Kati Thanda-
Lake Eyre   4

Cape of
Good Hope   R. Darling

R. Murray   New   40° S

Tasman
Sea   Zealand

3

60° S

S O U T H E R N   O C E A N

Antarctic Circle

A N T A R C T I C A   H   I   J   2

40° E   80° E   120° E   160° E   80° S

South America   Antarctica   Europe   Oceania

Total population of Europe
(excluding Russia)
595 million

Key to symbols

◤ Countries
■ Capital city
○ Important city/town

1 BELGIUM
2 BOSNIA AND HERZEGOVINA
3 KOSOVO
4 LIECHTENSTEIN
5 LUXEMBOURG
6 MONTENEGRO
7 NETHERLANDS
8 SLOVENIA
9 SWITZERLAND

Russia
Area 17 million sq km
Population 143 million

Country with most people
(excluding Russia)
Germany 81 million

Largest country
(excluding Russia)
Ukraine 603 700 sq km

Largest city
(Western Europe)
Paris 11 million

Largest city
Istanbul 12 million

ARCTIC OCEAN

Spitsbergen

Novaya Zemlya

White Sea

ATLANTIC OCEAN

Jan Mayen (Norway)

ICELAND
■ Reykjavík

Faroe Islands (Denmark)

RUSSIA

N O R W A Y
S W E D E N
F I N L A N D

Gulf of Bothnia

Oslo ■
Stockholm ■
Helsinki ■
Tallinn ■
ESTONIA
LATVIA
Riga ■
St Petersburg ○
Moscow ■

North Sea
Edinburgh ○
Belfast ○
Dublin ■
UNITED KINGDOM
IRELAND
London ■

DENMARK
Copenhagen ■
Baltic Sea
LITHUANIA
Vilnius ■
Minsk ■
RUSSIA
BELARUS

Amsterdam ■
The Hague 7
Brussels 1
5
GERMANY
Berlin ■
Warsaw ■
POLAND
Kiev ■
UKRAINE
Volgograd ○

English Channel
Paris ■
Prague ■
CZECH REPUBLIC
Munich ○
Vienna ■
SLOVAKIA
Bratislava ■
MOLDOVA
Chişinău ■
Odesa ○

FRANCE
Bern ■
9
4
AUSTRIA
Budapest ■
HUNGARY
ROMANIA
Bucharest ■
Black Sea

Bay of Biscay
Lyon ○
Ljubljana ■
8
Zagreb ■
Belgrade ■
Milan ○
CROATIA
Sarajevo ■
2
SERBIA
BULGARIA
Sofia ■
SAN MARINO
MONACO
ANDORRA
Corsica
6
3
Skopje ■
MACEDONIA
Istanbul ○
TURKEY

PORTUGAL
Lisbon ■
Madrid ■
SPAIN
Barcelona ○
Balearic Islands
Rome ■
ITALY
Adriatic Sea
Tirana ■
ALBANIA
Aegean Sea
Caspian Sea

Gibraltar (UK)
Strait of Gibraltar
Sardinia
Sicily
Crete
Rhodes
GREECE
Athens ■
ASIA

Mediterranean Sea

AFRICA
MALTA

The Colosseum, in Rome, was once used for gladiator fights.

The Arc de Triomphe in France's capital city, Paris.

0 250 500 750 1000 1250 km

Scale : One centimetre on this map is the same as 250 kilometres on the ground.

Key to symbols

- Lake
- Seasonal lake
- River
- Ice cap
- Mountain and height in metres — Mount Elbrus ▲ 5642

Land height above sea level in metres
- over 5000
- 2000 – 5000
- 1000 – 2000
- 500 – 1000
- 200 – 500
- 0 – 200

Land below sea level

Total area of Europe
10 million sq km

Largest island
Great Britain 218 476 sq km

Longest river
Volga 3688 km

Highest mountain
Mount Elbrus 5642 m

Largest lake
Caspian Sea 371 000 sq km

Map labels

ARCTIC OCEAN
Spitsbergen
Novaya Zemlya
ASIA
North Cape
Kola Peninsula
Lappland
White Sea
R. Pechora
Ural Mountains
Scandinavia
Lofoten Is
Gulf of Bothnia
Lake Onega
R. Northern Dvina
R. Sukhona
Jan Mayen
ATLANTIC OCEAN
Iceland
Faroe Islands
Shetland Islands
Orkney Islands
British Isles
Ireland
Great Britain
North Sea
Vänern
Vättern
Baltic Sea
Jutland
Lake Ladoga
Lake Peipus
R. Dvina
Central Russian Uplands
R. Volga
Volga Uplands
Caspian Lowland
North European Plain
R. Elbe
R. Vistula
R. Oder
R. Don
R. Donets
R. Dnieper
R. Volga
Caspian Sea
R. Thames
English Channel
R. Seine
R. Rhine
R. Loire
Sudeten Mts
R. Dniester
Carpathian Mountains
Caucasus
Mount Elbrus 5642
Black Sea
ASIA
Bay of Biscay
Cape Finisterre
Cantabrian Mts
Massif Central
Jura
Mont Blanc ▲ 4810
Alps
R. Rhône
Hungarian Plain
R. Danube
Pyrenees ▲ 3404
R. Duero
R. Ebro
R. Po
Dinaric Alps
Balkan Mts
Iberian Peninsula
R. Tagus
Corsica
Apennines
Adriatic Sea
Balearic Islands
Sardinia
Pindus Mts
Aegean Sea
Rhodes
Cape St Vincent
Sierra Nevada
Strait of Gibraltar
Mediterranean Sea
Mount Etna ▲ 3323
Sicily
Crete
Malta
AFRICA

N W E S

Mount Etna, on the island of Sicily, is one of the world's most active volcanoes.

Narrow, steep sided inlets called fjords are found along the Norwegian coastline.

0   250   500   750   1000   1250 km

Scale : One centimetre on this map is the same as 250 kilometres on the ground.

The headquarters of the EU in Brussels.

The European Union (EU) was created in 1957 by the Treaty of Rome. The original members of the then European Economic Community (EEC) were Belgium, France, West Germany, Italy, Luxembourg and the Netherlands. Since 1957 the EU has grown and now has 28 member states. The total population of the EU is now over half a billion.

European Union

- EU member
- EU candidate
- Non EU member

B.H.	BOSNIA AND HERZEGOVINA
KOS.	KOSOVO
L.	LIECHTENSTEIN
LUX.	LUXEMBOURG
MAC.	MACEDONIA
MOL.	MOLDOVA
MON.	MONTENEGRO
R.	RUSSIA
SL.	SLOVENIA
SWITZ.	SWITZERLAND

ICELAND

NORWAY
SWEDEN
FINLAND
ESTONIA
LATVIA
LITHUANIA
R.
DENMARK
UNITED KINGDOM
IRELAND
NETHERLANDS
BELGIUM
LUX.
GERMANY
POLAND
BELARUS
UKRAINE
CZECH REPUBLIC
SLOVAKIA
FRANCE
SWITZ.
L.
AUSTRIA
HUNGARY
MOL.
SL.
ROMANIA
CROATIA
B.H.
SERBIA
MON.
KOS.
MAC.
BULGARIA
ANDORRA
ITALY
ALBANIA
PORTUGAL
SPAIN
TURKEY
GREECE
MALTA
CYPRUS

Austria
Belgium
Bulgaria
Croatia
Cyprus
Czech Republic
Denmark
Estonia
Finland
France
Germany
Greece
Hungary
Ireland
Italy
Latvia
Lithuania
Luxembourg
Malta
Netherlands
Poland
Portugal
Romania
Slovakia
Slovenia
Spain
Sweden
United Kingdom

Key to symbols

- Countries
- ■ Capital city
- ○ Important city/town

N
W · E
S

Shetland
Islands

Orkney
Islands

ATLANTIC
OCEAN

Outer Hebrides

Inverness

Aberdeen

Fort William

SCOTLAND

Dundee

North

Sea

Glasgow ■ **Edinburgh**

Londonderry
(Derry)

**NORTHERN
IRELAND** ■ **Belfast**

Newcastle
upon Tyne

UNITED

Middlesbrough

Isle of
Man

York

Dundalk

Blackpool   Bradford Leeds

IRELAND

Preston

Irish Sea

Manchester

Liverpool   Sheffield

Galway   **Dublin** ■

KINGDOM

Limerick

Stoke-on-Trent   Derby   Nottingham

E N G L A N D   Norwich

Waterford

Wolverhampton   Leicester
Birmingham
Coventry   Cambridge

WALES

Ipswich

Cork

Oxford

Celtic Sea

Swansea   Bristol   Reading   London ■   Southend-on-Sea

Cardiff ■

BELGIUM

Southampton   Brighton
Portsmouth
Bournemouth

Plymouth   Torquay

English Channel

Channel
Islands

FRANCE

Tower Bridge crosses the River Thames in London.

Scale : One centimetre on this map is the same as 50 kilometres on the ground.

Area recorded by satellite

Satellite

Direction of earth's rotation

Orbit of satellite around earth

Earth

Satellite images are recorded by sensors similar to television cameras which are carried aboard satellites. These satellites orbit 500 km above the earth and images are beamed back to earth.

Snow covered mountains in Scotland.

Mountains covered with heather and poor grass.

Much of the land in the UK is used for agriculture. This is why so much of the image shows greens and browns.

The image above is a simulated natural colour image of Great Britain and Ireland. The image was made on a clear, cloudless day so a lot of detail is visible. Notice the Shetland Islands in the far north, and the Orkney Islands south of them closer to the coast. The island of Skye off the west coast of Scotland also stands out clearly.

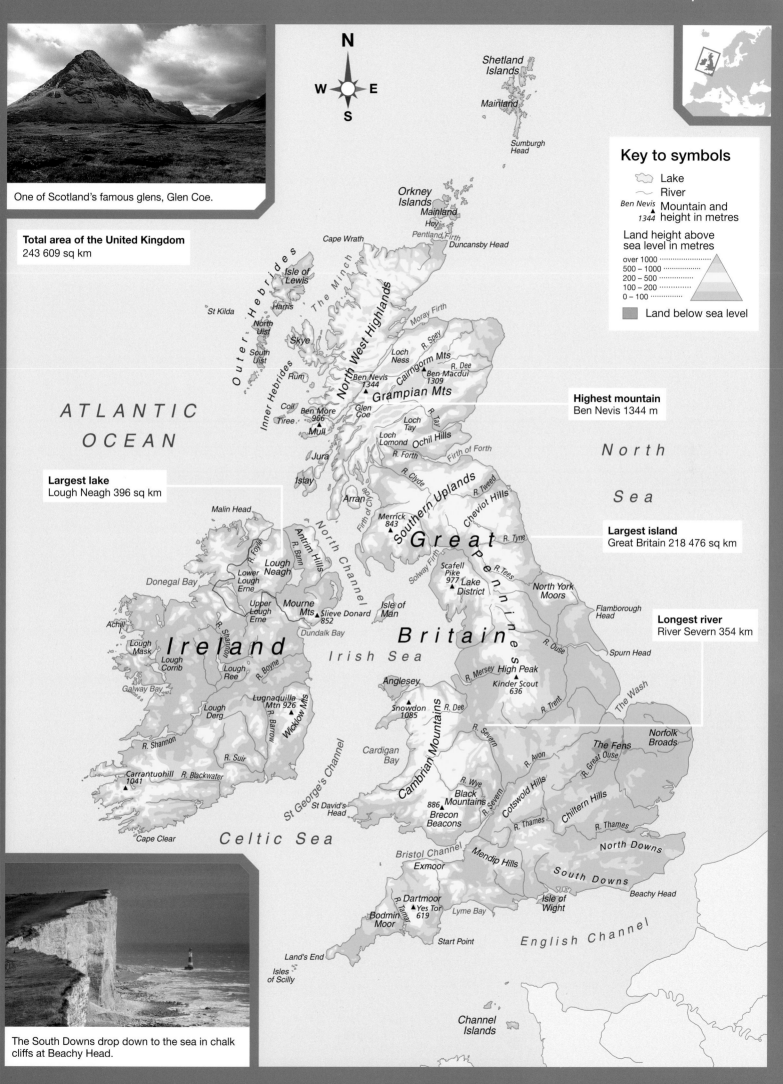

One of Scotland's famous glens, Glen Coe.

Total area of the United Kingdom
243 609 sq km

Key to symbols

Lake
River
Ben Nevis ▲ Mountain and
1344 height in metres

Land height above
sea level in metres
over 1000 ....
500 – 1000 ....
200 – 500 ....
100 – 200 ....
0 – 100 ....

Land below sea level

Highest mountain
Ben Nevis 1344 m

Largest lake
Lough Neagh 396 sq km

Largest island
Great Britain 218 476 sq km

Longest river
River Severn 354 km

N
W E
S

A T L A N T I C
O C E A N

N o r t h

S e a

Shetland
Islands
Mainland

Sumburgh
Head

Orkney
Islands
Mainland
Hoy
Pentland Firth
Duncansby Head

Cape Wrath

Isle of
Lewis

St Kilda

Harris

North
Uist

Skye

South
Uist

Rum

Coll

Tiree

Mull

Ben More
966 ▲

Jura

Islay

Arran

Outer Hebrides

Inner Hebrides

The Minch

North West Highlands

Moray Firth

R. Spey

Loch
Ness

Cairngorm Mts

Ben Macdui
1309 ▲

R. Dee

Ben Nevis
1344 ▲

Grampian Mts

Glen
Coe

Loch
Tay

R. Tay

Loch
Lomond

Ochil Hills

R. Forth

Firth of Forth

R. Clyde

Firth of Clyde

Southern Uplands

R. Tweed

Cheviot Hills

Merrick
843 ▲

Solway Firth

G r e a t

R. Tyne

Malin Head

Donegal Bay

Achill
I.

Lough
Mask

Lough
Corrib

Galway Bay

Lough
Derg

R. Shannon

R. Blackwater

Carrantuohill
1041 ▲

Cape Clear

R. Foyle

R. Bann

Antrim Hills

Lough
Neagh

Lower
Lough
Erne

Upper
Lough
Erne

Mourne
Mts
Slieve Donard
852 ▲

Dundalk Bay

North Channel

I r e l a n d

Lugnaquilla
Mtn 926 ▲

Wicklow Mts

Lough
Ree

R. Boyne

R. Barrow

R. Suir

Lough
Neagh

I r i s h   S e a

Isle of
Man

B r i t a i n

Scafell
Pike
977 ▲

Lake
District

North York
Moors

Flamborough
Head

Spurn Head

The Wash

Norfolk
Broads

P e n n i n e s

R. Tees

R. Ouse

R. Mersey

High Peak

Kinder Scout
636

R. Trent

Anglesey

Snowdon
1085 ▲

Cambrian Mountains

Cardigan
Bay

R. Dee

R. Severn

R. Wye

Black
Mountains
886 ▲

Brecon
Beacons

R. Severn

Cotswold Hills

Chiltern Hills

The Fens

R. Great Ouse

R. Avon

R. Thames

R. Thames

North Downs

South Downs

Beachy Head

Isle of
Wight

St George's Channel

*St David's
Head*

C e l t i c   S e a

Bristol Channel

Exmoor

Mendip Hills

Bodmin
Moor

Dartmoor
Yes Tor
619 ▲

R. Tamar

Lyme Bay

Start Point

E n g l i s h   C h a n n e l

Land's End

Isles
of Scilly

Channel
Islands

The South Downs drop down to the sea in chalk cliffs at Beachy Head.

Scale : One centimetre on this map is the same as 20 kilometres on the ground.

0 20 40 60 80 100 km

Key to symbols

Countries		Airport
■ Capital city	⊕	Lake
○ Main city/town		River
○ Other city/town	*Snowdon*	Mountain and
— Road	▲ 1085	height in metres
Railway		

England
Capital : London

Wales
Capital : Cardiff

Guernsey
Capital : St Peter Port

Isle of Man
Capital : Douglas

Jersey
Capital : St Helier

United Kingdom
Capital : London

1 Isles of Scilly

FRANCE

Channel Islands
Alderney
Guernsey St Peter Port Sark
Jersey St Helier

English Channel

Cherbourg
Bayeux

WALES

Cambrian Mountains
Newtown
Llandindod Wells
Brecon Beacons
Brecon
Ebbw Vale
Pontypool
Merthyr Tydfil
Rhondda
Neath
Caerphilly
Port-Talbot
Swansea
Bridgend
Newport
Cardiff
Barry
Weston-super-Mare

Aberystwyth
Aberaeron
Carmarthen
R. Tywi
R. Teifi
Pembroke
Haverfordwest
Milford Haven
Fishguard
St David's Head

Bristol Channel
Ilfracombe
Barnstaple
Bideford
Bude
Hartland Point
R. Taw
Exmoor
Bridgwater
Taunton
Tiverton
R. Exe
Exeter
Newton Abbot
Dartmoor
R. Tamar
Launceston
Bodmin
Newquay
Truro
Redruth
Camborne
Penzance
Land's End
Lizard Point
St Austell
Falmouth
Plymouth
Brixham
Torquay
Teignmouth
Exmouth
Sidmouth

Lyme Bay
North Dorset Downs
Dorchester
Weymouth
Bill of Portland

Mendip Hills
Bath
Bristol
Gloucester
Hereford
R. Wye
R. Teme
Kidderminster
Worcester
Bromsgrove
Dudley
West Bromwich
Birmingham
Coventry
Warwick
R. Avon
Stratford-upon-Avon
Rugby
Corby
Kettering
Northampton
Bedford
Cheltenham
Cotswold Hills
Royal Wootton Bassett
R. Thames
Witney
Oxford
Bicester
Milton Keynes
Luton
R. Cherwell
Swindon
Newbury
R. Kennet
R. Test
Salisbury Plain
Andover
Frome
Yeovil
Salisbury
Winchester
Eastleigh
Southampton
Isle of Wight
Newport
Portsmouth
Bournemouth
Poole
Chichester
South Downs
Bognor Regis
Brighton
Worthing
Crawley
Reigate
Guildford
Woking
Basingstoke
Reading
Maidenhead
Hemel Hempstead
Watford
Slough
London
Bromley
Croydon
Barnet
Stevenage
Hertford
Harlow
Cambridge
R. Great Ouse
The Fens
Thetford
Newmarket
Bury St Edmunds
Ipswich
Felixstowe
Harwich
Lowestoft
Colchester
Clacton-on-Sea
Chelmsford
Basildon
Southend-on-Sea
Gillingham
Gravesend
Dartford
Maidstone
Royal Tunbridge Wells
The Weald
Hayward's Heath
Newhaven
Eastbourne
Beachy Head
Hastings
Dungeness
Folkestone
Ashford
Canterbury
Dover
Strait of Dover
Ramsgate
Boulogne-sur-Mer

English Channel

St George's Channel
Bay

2
1
E
D
C
B
A

Scotland
Capital : Edinburgh

Shetland Islands

Unst
Yell
Foula
Mainland
Lerwick
Bressay
Sumburgh Head
Fair Isle
60° N

North Ronaldsay
Westray
Sanday
Orkney Islands
Mainland
Kirkwall
Hoy
South Ronaldsay
John o'Groats

Cape Wrath
Durness
Thurso
Wick
Helmsdale

Butt of Lewis
Stornoway
Isle of Lewis
Harris
The Minch
Lochinver
Ullapool
An Teallach 1062

Outer Hebrides
Lochmaddy
North Uist
Uig
Portree
Skye
Kyle of Lochalsh

North West Highlands
Invergordon
Dingwall
Inverness
Loch Ness
Fort Augustus
Aviemore
Ben Macdui 1309

Dornoch Firth
Moray Firth
Elgin
Nairn
Banff
Fraserburgh
Rattray Head
Peterhead
Huntly
R. Spey
R. Deveron
R. Don
Aberdeen
R. Dee

South Uist
Lochboisdale
Barra
Inner Hebrides
Rum
Eigg
Mallaig
Fort William
Ben Nevis 1344

Grampian Mountains
R. North Esk
R. South Esk
Blair Atholl
Pitlochry
Brechin
Montrose
Forfar
Arbroath
Stonehaven

Coll
Tobermory
Tiree
Mull
Oban
Firth of Lorn
Crianlarich
Ben More 1174
R. Tay
Loch Tay
SCOTLAND
Blairgowrie
Dundee
Perth
Firth of Tay
St Andrews

North Sea

ATLANTIC OCEAN

Colonsay
Jura
Inveraray
Lochgilphead
R. Forth
Loch Lomond
Stirling
Ochil Hills
Glenrothes
Kirkcaldy
Dunfermline
Firth of Forth
Dunbar

Greenock
Dumbarton
Clydebank
Paisley
Glasgow
Motherwell
Hamilton
East Kilbride
Falkirk
Livingston
Edinburgh
Berwick-upon-Tweed

Port Askaig
Islay
Bute
Rothesay
Firth of Clyde
Irvine
Kilmarnock
Peebles
Galashiels
R. Tweed
Coldstream
Alnwick

Port Ellen
Arran
Ayr
Prestwick
R. Clyde
R. Teviot
Jedburgh
Hawick
Cheviot Hills

Campbeltown
Southern Uplands
Moffat
Morpeth
R. Tyne

Mull of Kintyre
North Channel
Girvan
Merrick 843
Lockerbie
South Shields

Antrim Hills
NORTHERN IRELAND
Ballymena
Larne
Stranraer
Newton Stewart
Castle Douglas
Dumfries
Longtown
Carlisle
Newcastle upon Tyne
Sunderland
Durham

Lough Neagh
Antrim
Newtownabbey
Bangor
Belfast
Whithorn
Solway Firth
Workington
ENGLAND
Lake District
R. Wear
Bishop Auckland
R. Tees
Stockton-on-Tees
Penrith

Key to symbols

- Countries
- ■ Capital city
- ○ Main city/town
- ○ Other city/town
- — Road
- ⊢ Railway
- ✈ Airport
- Lake
- River
- ▲ *Ben Nevis 1344* Mountain and height in metres

8° W 6° W 4° W 2° W

Scale : One centimetre on this map is the same as 20 kilometres on the ground.

0 20 40 60 80 100 km

Key to symbols

- Countries
- Capital city
- ○ Main city/town
- ○ Other city/town
- — Road
- Railway
- ✈ Airport
- Lake
- River
- *Carrantuohill* ▲ 1041 Mountain and height in metres

SCOTLAND

Port Askaig
Islay
Jura
Rothesay
Bute
Irvine
Port Ellen
Arran
Prestwick
Ayr
Campbeltown
Mull of Kintyre
Girvan
Stranraer

North Channel
Firth of Clyde

Malin Head
Bloody Foreland
Errigal ▲ 752
Letterkenny
Lough Foyle
Portrush
Coleraine
Antrim Hills
Larne

NORTHERN

Londonderry (Derry)
Strabane
Ballymena
R. Bann
Antrim

Donegal
Omagh
Cookstown
Lough Neagh
Newtownabbey
Bangor
Belfast

IRELAND

Dungannon
R. Lagan
Lisburn

Donegal Bay
Lower Lough Erne
Enniskillen
Armagh
Downpatrick
Isle of Man

Erris Head
Belmullet
Sligo
Upper Lough Erne
Monaghan
Newry
Newcastle
▲ 852 Slieve Donard
Mourne Mts

Ballina
Lough Allen
Dundalk

Lough Conn
Carrick-on-Shannon
Cavan
Dundalk Bay

Achill Island
Castlebar
Charlestown
Drogheda

Westport
Lough Mask
Claremorris
Longford
Lough Ree
Navan
R. Boyne
Skerries
Irish Sea

Connemara
Lough Corrib
Roscommon
R. Suck
Mullingar

Galway
Athlone
R. Shannon
Dublin
Dún Laoghaire

Galway Bay
IRELAND
Tullamore
R. Liffey
Bray
Naas
Wicklow Mts

Aran Islands
Lough Derg
Portlaoise
R. Barrow
Wicklow
Wicklow Head

ATLANTIC OCEAN

Roscrea
Ennis
Nenagh
Carlow
Arklow

Kilkee
Kilrush
Thurles
R. Nore
Kilkenny

Limerick
R. Suir
Enniscorthy

Tipperary
Cahir
Carrick-on-Suir
New Ross
Wexford
Rosslare

Tralee
Clonmel
Waterford

Dingle
Mallow
R. Blackwater
Fermoy
Knockmealdown Mts
Dungarvan

Killarney
Carrantuohill ▲ 1041
R. Lee
Youghal
Fishguard

Dingle Bay
Boggeragh Mts
Cork
Cobh
WALES

Sneem
Bantry
St David's Head
Haverfordwest

Skibbereen
Old Head of Kinsale
Milford Haven

Mizen Head
Cape Clear
Pembroke

St George's Channel

Celtic Sea

Ireland
Capital : Dublin

Northern Ireland
Capital : Belfast

10° W   8° W   6° W

54° N   52° N

0   20   40   60   80   100 km

Scale : One centimetre on this map is the same as 20 kilometres on the ground.

A   B   C   D   E   F   G   H   I   J

25°W   20°W   15°W   10°W   5°W   0°   5°E   10°E   15°E   20°E

N W E S

6

Arctic Circle

65°N

I C E L A N D

Akureyri

Surtsey   ⊕ ■Reykjavik   Vatnajökull   Seyðisfjörður

Tromsø

Lofoten Islands

Narvik

Bodø

5

N o r w e g i a n   S e a

60°N

Faroe Islands (Denmark)

Trondheim

Ålesund

Galdhøpiggen ▲ 2470   Lillehammer

Bergen

Östersund

Sundsvall

Umeå

Gulf of

Key to symbols

◣ Countries
■ Capital city
○ Main city/town
○ Other city/town
— Road
⊞ Railway
〜 Canal
⊕ Airport
⬭ Lake
〜 River
Galdhøpiggen ▲ 2470   Mountain and height in metres

Shetland Islands

A T L A N T I C   O C E A N

Outer Hebrides

Orkney Islands

Inverness

Ben Nevis 1344   Grampian Mountains   Aberdeen

Glasgow

Londonderry (Derry)

N o r t h   S e a

Drammen   ⊕ ■Oslo

Stavanger

Kristiansand

Karlstad

Vänern

Uppsala

Västerås

Örebro   **Stockho**

Norrköping

55°N

Edinburgh

Dundee

U N I T E D

Newcastle upon Tyne

Gothenburg

Aalborg

Skagerrak

Vättern

Jönköping

Gotland

4

50°N

Galway

I R E L A N D

Limerick

Cork

Belfast

Carlisle

Irish Sea

Blackpool   Liverpool

Wexford

K I N G D O M

Leeds

Manchester

Sheffield

Birmingham

Nottingham

Kattegat

Öland

Karlskrona

DENMARK

Aarhus

Esbjerg

Copenhagen

Odense   ■ Malmö

Bornholm

B a l t i c

3

Swansea

Cardiff

Plymouth

Oxford   Norwich

R.Thames

Bristol   ⊕ ■London   Dover   Bruges

Southampton   Strait of Dover

English Channel   Calais

NETHERLANDS

■Amsterdam

The Hague   IJsselmeer

Rotterdam

Eindhoven

Antwerp   **BELGIUM**   Essen

Lille   ■**Brussels**   Düsseldorf

Liège   Cologne

Bonn

Groningen

Bremen

Hannover

Bielefeld

Duisburg   Dortmund

R.Elbe

Kiel

Hamburg   Rostock

R.Weser

Magdeburg

GERMANY

R.Elbe

■**Berlin**

Gdańsk

Szczecin   Koszalin

Bydgoszcz

Poznań

R.Oder

POLA

2

Channel Islands

Brest

Rennes

Le Havre   Amiens   Rouen

Caen   R.Seine

LUXEMBOURG

■**Luxembourg**

Reims   Mainz

Nancy

R.Rhine

Frankfurt

Erfurt

Leipzig

Dresden

Zielona Góra

Wrocław

Sudeten Mts.

Katov

1

La Rochelle

Nantes   R.Loire   Tours

Le Mans   Orléans   R.Loire

Poitiers   R.Seine

F R A N C E

Dijon

Strasbourg

Basel

Zürich   ⊕ **Bern**   **SWITZERLAND** 10°E

Karlsruhe

Stuttgart

Nuremberg

Plzeň

Nancy

R.Rhine   R.Danube

Munich   R.Inn

Innsbruck

Salzburg   **LIECHTENSTEIN**

■**Prague**

CZECH REPUBLIC

Brno

Linz

■**Vienna**   **Bratislav**

AUSTRIA   Graz   **HUN**

Ostrava

SLO

Budapes

45°N

5°W   0°   5°E   10°E   15°E

E   F   G   H   I   J

0   100   200   300   400   500 km

Scale : One centimetre on this map is the same as 100 kilometres on the ground.

Czech Republic J2
Capital : Prague

Denmark H4
Capital : Copenhagen

Estonia K4
Capital : Tallinn

Finland K5
Capital : Helsinki

Germany H3
Capital : Berlin

Iceland B5
Capital : Reykjavík

Ireland E3
Capital : Dublin

Latvia K4
Capital : Riga

Liechtenstein H2
Capital : Vaduz

Lithuania K4
Capital : Vilnius

Luxembourg H2
Capital : Luxembourg

Netherlands G3
Capital : Amsterdam / The Hague

Norway H5
Capital : Oslo

Poland J3
Capital : Warsaw

Sweden I4
Capital : Stockholm

United Kingdom F4
Capital : London

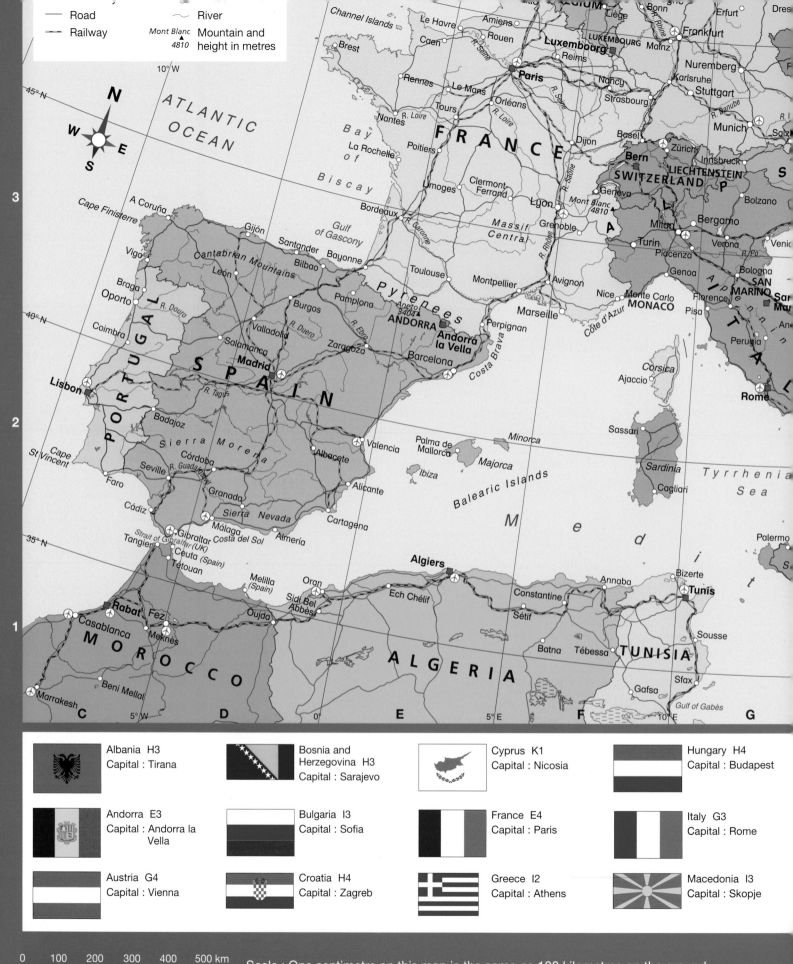

Road
Railway
Mont Blanc ▲ 4810 Mountain and height in metres
River

ATLANTIC OCEAN

45° N
40° N
35° N

10° W
5° W
0°
5° E
10° E

FRANCE

Channel Islands
Le Havre
Amiens
Rouen
Caen
Brest
Rennes
Le Mans
Nantes
Tours
Orléans
Poitiers
La Rochelle
Bordeaux
Limoges
Clermont-Ferrand
Lyon
Grenoble
Montpellier
Avignon
Nice
Marseille
Perpignan
Toulouse
Bayonne

Bay of Biscay
Gulf of Gascony

R. Seine
R. Loire
R. Loire
R. Garonne
R. Saône
R. Rhône

Paris
Reims
Nancy
Strasbourg
Dijon

Massif Central

Mont Blanc ▲ 4810

Côte d'Azur
Monte Carlo
MONACO

Luxembourg
LUXEMBOURG
Mainz
Frankfurt
Erfurt
Dres
Bonn
Liège
Nuremberg
Karlsruhe
Stuttgart
Munich
Salz
R. R

SWITZERLAND
Bern
Geneva
Zürich
Basel
Innsbruck
LIECHTENSTEIN
Bolzano
Bergamo
Verona
Venic
R. Po
Milan
Turin
Piacenza
Genoa
Bologna
SAN MARINO
Sar
Ma
Florence
Pisa
Perugia
Ane

I T A L Y
Rome
Corsica
Ajaccio
Sardinia
Sassari
Cagliari

Tyrrhenian Sea

Palermo
S

PORTUGAL
SPAIN

A Coruña
Cape Finisterre
Vigo
Braga
Oporto
Coimbra
Lisbon
Cape St Vincent
Faro
Cádiz
Gijón
Santander
Bilbao
Cantabrian Mountains
León
Braga
R. Douro
R. Duero
Valladolid
Salamanca
Burgos
Pamplona
Zaragoza
Aneto 3404
ANDORRA
Andorra la Vella
Barcelona
Costa Brava

Madrid
Badajoz
Sierra Morena
Córdoba
Seville
R. Guadalquivir
Granada
Sierra Nevada
Málaga Costa del Sol
Almería
Gibraltar (UK)
Strait of Gibraltar
Tangier
Ceuta (Spain)
Tétouan
Melilla (Spain)

Pyrenees

R. Ebro

R. Tagus

Albacete
Valencia
Alicante
Cartagena

Palma de Mallorca
Minorca
Majorca
Ibiza
Balearic Islands

M e d i t e r r a n e a n

Algiers
Oran
Sidi Bel Abbès
Ech Chélif
Constantine
Sétif
Annaba
Bizerte
Tunis
Sousse

MOROCCO
Rabat
Casablanca
Fez
Meknès
Oujda
Beni Mellal
Marrakesh

A L G E R I A
Batna
Tébessa
Gafsa
Sfax
Gulf of Gabès

TUNISIA

	Albania H3	Capital : Tirana
	Andorra E3	Capital : Andorra la Vella
	Austria G4	Capital : Vienna
	Bosnia and Herzegovina H3	Capital : Sarajevo
	Bulgaria I3	Capital : Sofia
	Croatia H4	Capital : Zagreb
	Cyprus K1	Capital : Nicosia
	France E4	Capital : Paris
	Greece I2	Capital : Athens
	Hungary H4	Capital : Budapest
	Italy G3	Capital : Rome
	Macedonia I3	Capital : Skopje

---

0 100 200 300 400 500 km

Scale : One centimetre on this map is the same as 100 kilometres on the ground.

 Malta G2
Capital : Valletta

 Portugal C2
Capital : Lisbon

 Slovakia H4
Capital : Bratislava

Switzerland F4
Capital : Bern

 Moldova J4
Capital : Chișinău

 Romania I4
Capital : Bucharest

 Slovenia G4
Capital : Ljubljana

 Turkey J2
Capital : Ankara

 Montenegro H3
Capital : Podgorica

 Serbia I3
Capital : Belgrade

 Spain C3
Capital : Madrid

 Ukraine J4
Capital : Kiev

The British Isles at the same scale.

Largest country
Russia 17 million sq km

Country with most people
China 1384 million

Total population of Asia
(including Russia)
4538 million

N
W E
S

A R C T I C   O C E A N

EUROPE

Russia
Area 17 million sq km
Population 143 million

St Petersburg

Moscow

Perm

Chelyabinsk

Omsk

Novosibirsk

Yakutsk

Sea of
Okhotsk

Sakhalin

Irkutsk
Lake
Baikal

Sapporo

R U S S I A

Volgograd

Black
Sea

Ankara
TURKEY
CYPRUS
GEORGIA
Tbilisi
Yerevan
Baku
2 2
LEBANON
ISRAEL
SYRIA
Damascus
Amman
JORDAN
Baghdad
IRAQ
Tehran
Ashgabat
KUWAIT
Kuwait
IRAN
Kabul
AFGHANISTAN
Islamabad
Lahore
PAKISTAN
Delhi

K A Z A K H S T A N
Astana

Aral
Sea
UZBEKISTAN
TURKMENISTAN
Tashkent
Dushanbe
3
Bishkek
4
Almaty

Lake
Balkhash

Ürümqi

M O N G O L I A
Ulan
Bator

Harbin
Shenyang
Pyongyang
NORTH
KOREA
Beijing
Tianjin
Seoul
SOUTH
KOREA

Sea of
Japan
(East
Sea)

JAPAN
Tokyo
Kobe Osaka
Fukuoka

Lanzhou
Xi'an
Nanjing
Shanghai

C H I N A

Wuhan

Chongqing

Largest city
Tokyo 38 million

Caspian Sea

Riyadh
BAHRAIN
QATAR
UNITED
ARAB
EMIRATES
Muscat
SAUDI
ARABIA
Karachi
OMAN

Red
Sea

Sanaa
YEMEN
Aden

N E P A L
New
Delhi
Kathmandu
Thimphu
BHUTAN
BANGLADESH
Dhaka
I N D I A
Kolkata
Mumbai
Hyderabad
Yangon
MYANMAR
(BURMA)
Nay Pyi Taw

Guangzhou
Hong
Kong

Taipei (Taibei)
TAIWAN

PACIFIC
OCEAN

Luzon

Arabian
Sea

Socotra
(Yemen)

AFRICA

Bay
of
Bengal

Chennai

Andaman Is
(India)

SRI
LANKA
Sri Jayewardenepura Kotte
Colombo

MALDIVES

Hanoi
Vientiane
THAILAND
Bangkok
CAMBODIA
Phnom Penh
Ho Chi
Minh City

PHILIPPINES
Manila

South
China
Sea

Mindanao
Davao

BRUNEI

Nicobar Is
(India)

M A L A Y S I A
Kuala Lumpur
Putrajaya
Singapore
SINGAPORE
Borneo
Celebes

Sumatra
I N D O N E S I A
Makassar

Dili
EAST
TIMOR

INDIAN OCEAN

Jakarta
Java
Surabaya

Key to symbols

◢ Countries
■ Capital city
○ Important city/town

1 ARMENIA
2 AZERBAIJAN
3 TAJIKISTAN
4 KYRGYZSTAN

Shanghai is China's largest city.

A fruit stall in the Chinatown market, Kuala Lumpur, Malaysia.

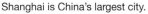

0   500   1000   1500   2000   2500 km

Scale : One centimetre on this map is the same as 500 kilometres on the ground.

Total area of Asia
45 million sq km

Largest lake
Caspian Sea 371 000 sq km

N
W   E
S

A R C T I C   O C E A N

*Central
Siberian
Plateau*

R. Lena

*Sea of
Okhotsk*

E U R O P E

Ural Mountains

R. Yenisey

R. Ob

*West
Siberian
Plain*

S i b e r i a

Sakhalin

Black Sea

*Caspian
Lowland*

Caucasus

R. Angara

R. Lena

R. Amur

Hokkaido

*Aral
Sea*

*Lake
Balkhash*

R. Irtysh

R. Yenisey

*Lake
Baikal*

R. Argun

R. Selenga

*Sea of
Japan
(East Sea)*

*Caspian
Sea*

R. Tigris

*Elburz
Mountains*

Zagros Mountains

Ysyk-Köl

T i e n   S h a n

A l t a i   M t s

*G o b i
D e s e r t*

Honshu

R. Euphrates

Tarim Basin

Huang He

Kyushu

Hindu Kush

K2
8611 ▲

K u n l u n   S h a n

*East
China Sea*

Longest river
Chang Jiang 6380 km

*Red
Sea*

The Gulf

*Plateau of
Tibet*

Chang Jiang

Arabian

Peninsula

R. Indus

Thar Desert

H i m a l a y a

Annapurna
8091 ▲

▲ Mount
Everest
8848

R. Ganges

R. Irrawaddy

Taiwan

PACIFIC

OCEAN

Highest mountain
Mount Everest 8848 m

*Arabian
Sea*

Deccan

*B a y
o f
B e n g a l*

R. Mekong

*S o u t h
C h i n a
S e a*

Luzon

Philippines

Gulf of Aden

AFRICA

Sri Lanka

Mindanao

Largest island
Borneo 745 561 sq km

B o r n e o

Celebes

Key to symbols

🝰 Lake
🝰 Seasonal lake
〜 River
▢ Ice cap
Mount Everest ▲ 8848 Mountain and height in metres

Land height above
sea level in metres

over 5000 ....
2000 – 5000 ....
1000 – 2000 ....
500 – 1000 ....
200 – 500 ....
0 – 200 ....

▢ Land below sea level

S u m a t r a

J a v a

I N D I A N   O C E A N

Rice is grown on terraced hillsides on the Indonesian island of Bali.

Mount Everest on the border between China and Nepal.

Key to symbols

- Countries
- ■ Capital city
- ○ Main city/town
- ○ Other city/town
- — Road
- Railway
- Canal
- ⊕ Airport
- Lake
- River
- *Mount Elbrus* ▲ 5642 Mountain and height in metres

Scale : One centimetre on this map is the same as 200 kilometres on the ground.

0   200   400   600   800 km

Afghanistan F4
Capital : Kabul

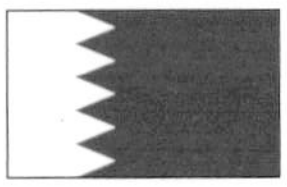

Bahrain E3
Capital : Manama

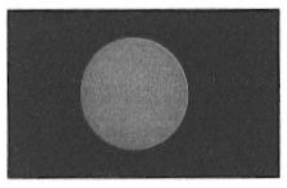

Bangladesh H3
Capital : Dhaka

Bhutan I3
Capital : Thimphu

India G3
Capital : New Delhi

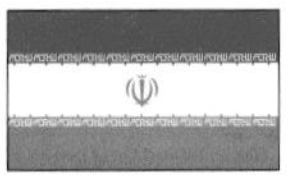

Iran E4
Capital : Tehran

Iraq D4
Capital : Baghdad

Israel C4
Capital : Jerusalem*

Jordan C4
Capital : Amman

Kuwait D3
Capital : Kuwait

Key to symbols
Countries
Capital city
Main city/town
Other city/town
Road
Railway
Canal
Airport
Lake
Seasonal lake
River
Mount Everest 8848
Mountain and height in metres
TURKEY
Ankara
Athens
Izmir
Antalya
Konya
Adana
Kayseri
Taurus Mts
Sivas
Erzurum
Samsun
Bat'umi
GEORGIA
Tbilisi
ARMENIA
Yerevan
Mt Ararat 5165
AZERBAIJAN
Baku
Gäncä
Makhachkala
Caspian Sea
Aktau
Ustyurt Plateau
Türkmenbaşy
TURKMENISTAN
Urgar
Mediterranean Sea
Crete
Rhodes
Nicosia
CYPRUS
LIBYA
Tobruk
Marsa Matruh
Al Jaghbub
Qattara Depression
Alexandria
Tanta
Cairo
Giza
Al Fayyum
Port Said
Suez Canal
Suez
Sinai
Beirut
LEBANON
Homs
Aleppo
Gaziantep
Malatya
Lake Van
SYRIA
Ar Raqqah
Mesopotamia
Damascus
ISRAEL
Tel Aviv-Yafo
Jerusalem
GAZA
Amman
JORDAN
Aqaba
Syrian Desert
Baghdad
IRAQ
Mosul
Erbil
Kermanshah
Tabriz
Rasht
Elburz Mountains
Gorgan
Karaj
Tehran
Qom
Sabzevar
Mashhad
Isfahan
IRAN
Yazd
Birjand
Zagros Mountains
Ahvaz
Basra
An Najaf
R. Tigris
R. Euphrates
Al Jawf
Tabuk
KUWAIT
Kuwait
Bushehr
Shiraz
Kerman
Zahedan
Bandar-e Abbas
EGYPT
Al Minya
Asyut
R. Nile
Qina
Luxor
Aswan
Hurghada
Al Qusayr
Hijaz
Tropic of Cancer
Lake Nasser
Wadi Halfa
SAUDI ARABIA
Buraydah
Medina
Riyadh
BAHRAIN
Manama
QATAR
Doha
The Gulf
Dubai
Abu Dhabi
UNITED ARAB EMIRATES
OMAN
Gulf of Oman
Muscat
Red Sea
Jeddah
Mecca
At Ta'if
Arabian Peninsula
Rub' al Khali
Asir
Abha
SUDAN
Merowe
Port Sudan
Atbara
R. Atbara
Masirah
Karora
ERITREA
Kassala
Massawa
Asmara
Sanaa
YEMEN
Hodeidah
Ta'izz
Mukalla
Salalah
Ras Dejen 4533
Gonder
Lake Tana
Assab
Aden
Gulf of Aden
Socotra (Yemen)
Cape Guardafui
DJIBOUTI
Djibouti
Ethiopian Highlands
Dire Dawa
Berbera
Addis Ababa
Hargeisa
ETHIOPIA
Shashemene
Wendo
Webi Shabeelle
Garoowe
SOMALIA
INDIA
30° N
20° N
10° N
30° E
40° E
50° E
60° E
C
D
E
1
2
3
4

Kyrgyzstan G5
Capital : Bishkek

Lebanon C4
Capital : Beirut

Nepal H3
Capital : Kathmandu

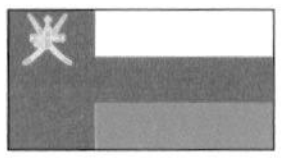

Oman E2
Capital : Muscat

Pakistan F3
Capital : Islamabad

Qatar E3
Capital : Doha

Saudi Arabia D3
Capital : Riyadh

* Internationally disputed capital.

0 200 400 600 800 km

Scale : One centimetre on this map is the same as 200 kilometres on the ground.

5

al'sk   Zhezkazgan   Balkhash   Lake
Balkhash   Aktogay
K A Z A K H S T A N

Kyzylorda   Zhezkazgan   Balkhash   Yining   Ürümqi
Karamay   M O N G O L I A

40° N

Almaty   Turpan   Laojunmiao   Yinchuan
R. Syr Darya   Shymkent   Bishkek   Ysyk-Köl   Korla   Lop Nur
Buxoro   Tashkent   KYRGYZSTAN   Tien   Shan   Aksu   Tarim He   Qinghai
Hu   Lanzhou   110° E
Qo'qon   Naryn   Kashi   Tarim   Basin

40° E

Türkmenabat   Samarqand   TAJIKISTAN   Hetan   Xining   Xi'an
Dushanbe   Tianshui   Hanzhong

Mazar-e
Sharif   Hindu Kush   Karakoram Range   K2
8611   K U N L U N   S H A N   C H I N A   Golmud   Mianyang   Wanxian
Chengdu   Nanchong
Kabul   Peshawar   R. Indus   Srinagar   Plateau
of Tibet   Nagqu   Qamdo   Gongga
Shan
7514   Leshan   Chongqing   30° N
AFGHANISTAN   Islamabad   H   Yibin
Rawalpindi   Gujranwala   Panzhihua   Lupanshui   Guiyang
Kandahar   Lahore   Amritsar   i   Xigazê   Lhasa   Nyingchi   Qujing
Quetta   Faisalabad   Ludhiana   m   8091   Lhazê   Chuxiong   Kaiyuan   3
Multan   R. Sutlej   a   Annapurna   8848   Dibrugarh   Myitkyina   Kunming   Tropic of Cancer
Nushki   R. Indus   Meerut   NEPAL   l   Mount
Everest   Thimphu   R. Brahmaputra   VIETNAM
PAKISTAN   Delhi   Ghaziabad   a   Darjiling   BHUTAN   Guwahati   Phongsali
Thar Desert   New Delhi   Bareilly   y   Kathmandu   MYANMAR   LAOS   Luangphabang
Hyderabad   Faridabad   Agra   Lucknow   Gorakhpur   a   (BURMA)   20° N
Ahmadabad   Jaipur   Kanpur   Patna   BANGLADESH   Mandalay
Jodhpur   Kota   R. Ganges   Varanasi   Dhanbad   Asansol   Dhaka   Meiktila   Nay Pyi Taw
Jhansi   Allahabad   Ranchi   Kolkata   Khulna   Chittagong   Myingyan   Pyinmana
Rajkot   Vadodara   Bhopal   Jabalpur   Jamshedpur   Kharagpur   Mouths of the
Ganges   Sittwe   Myaungmya   Vientiane
Bhavnagar   R. Narmada   Indore   INDIA   Sambalpur   Cuttack   Pye   Chiang
Mai   THAILAND
Surat   R. Tapi   Nagpur   Durg-
Bhilainagar   Sandoway   Bago   Khon Kaen
Nashik   Aurangabad   Western Ghats   Bay   Bassein   Yangon
(Rangoon)   Moulmein   Nakhon
Sawan   2
Arabian
Sea   Mumbai   Pune   Deccan   R. Godavari   of   Bangkok   Sisophon
Solapur   Nizamabad   Bengal   Rat Buri   Samut
Prakan
Warangal   R. Godavari   Vishakhapatnam   Mergui   Chanthaburi
Hyderabad   R. Krishna   Gulf
of
Thailand
Belagavi
(Belgaum)   Vijayawada   Andaman
Islands
(India)   Chumphon   10° N
Kurnool   Andaman
Sea   Ranong
Hubballi
(Hubli)   Eastern Ghats
Chitradurga   Chennai   Nakhon Si
Thammarat
Mangaluru
(Mangalore)   Bengaluru
(Bangalore)   Puducherry   Phuket
Salem   Songkhla   1
Kozhikode   Coimbatore   George
Town   MALAYSIA
Laccadive
Islands
(India)   Kochi   Madurai   Jaffna   Trincomalee   Nicobar Islands
(India)   Ipoh   Strait of Malacca   Kuala
Lumpur
Thiruvananthapuram   SRI LANKA   Banda Aceh   INDONESIA   Putrajaya
O C E A N   Kandy   Medan
MALDIVES   Colombo   Sri Jayewardenepura
Kotte

70° E   80° E   90° E

F   G   H   I

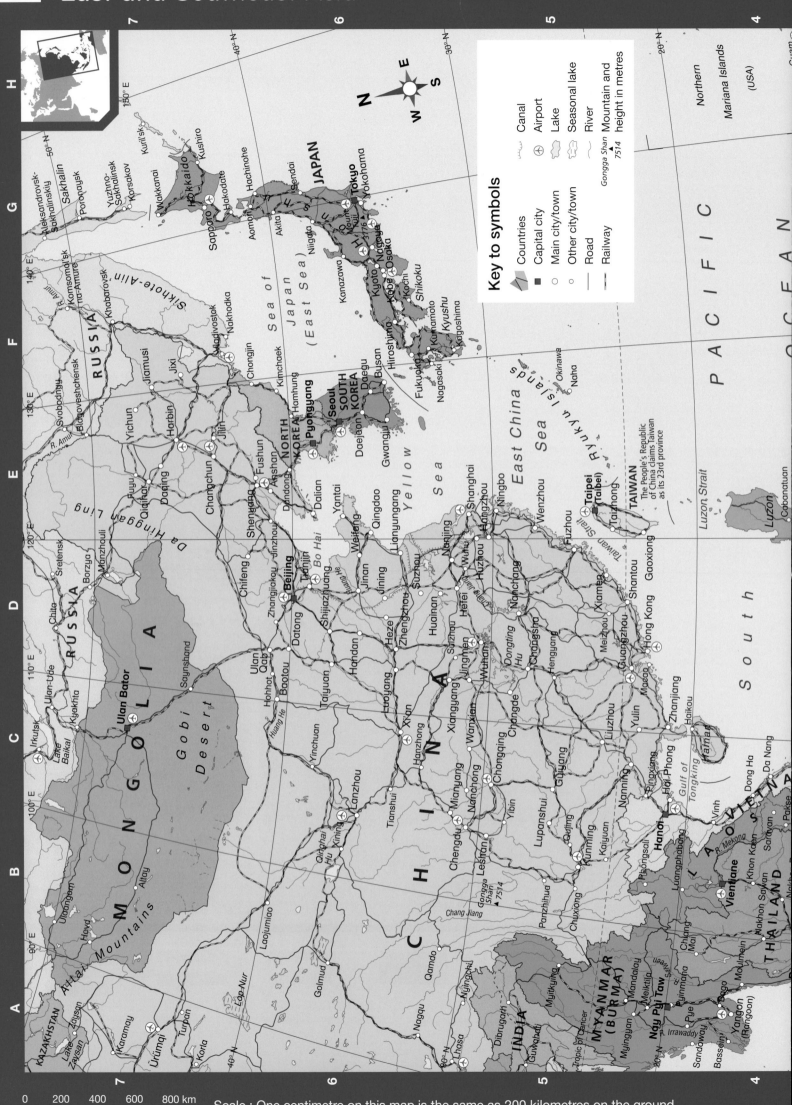

Key to symbols

Countries

Capital city

☐ Main city/town

○ Other city/town

— Road

Railway

Canal

⊕ Airport

Lake

Seasonal lake

River

Gongga Shan Mountain and
▲ 7514 height in metres

Scale : One centimetre on this map is the same as 200 kilometres on the ground.

0   200   400   600   800 km

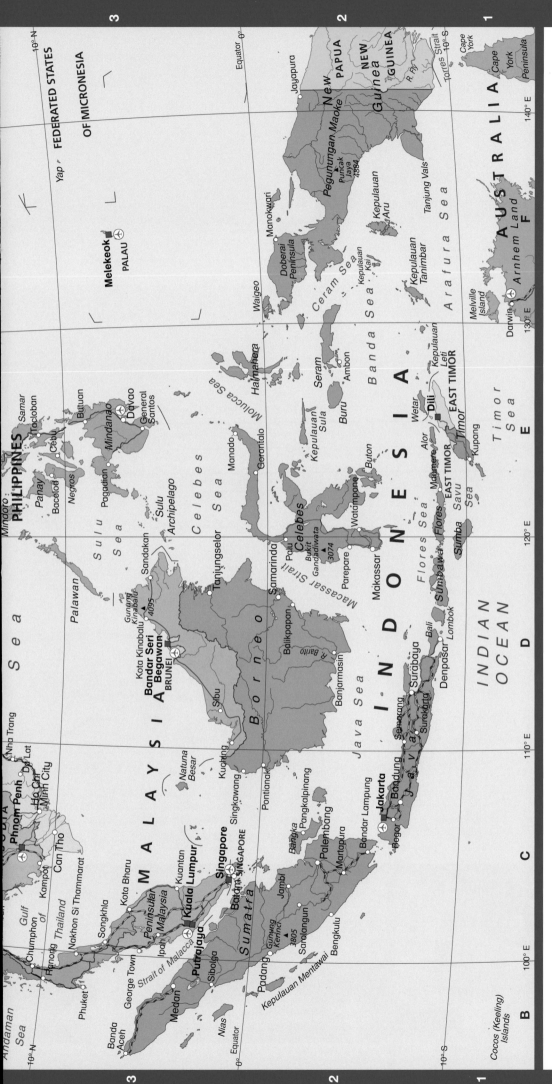

Mongolia B7
Capital : Ulan Bator

Vietnam C4
Capital : Hanoi

Malaysia C3
Capital :
Putrajaya /
Kuala Lumpur

Thailand B4
Capital : Bangkok

Laos C4
Capital : Vientiane

Taiwan E5
Capital : Taipei

Japan G6
Capital : Tokyo

South Korea E6
Capital : Seoul

Indonesia D2
Capital : Jakarta

Singapore C3
Capital : Singapore

East Timor E2
Capital : Dili

Philippines E4
Capital : Manila

China B6
Capital : Beijing

Palau F3
Capital : Melekeok

Cambodia C4
Capital :
Phnom Penh

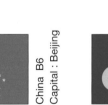
North Korea E7
Capital :
Pyongyang

Brunei D3
Capital : Bandar
Seri Begawan

Myanmar B4
Capital :
Nay Pyi Taw

Total population
of North America
574 million

Key to symbols
- Countries
- ■ Capital city
- ○ Important city/town

ARCTIC
OCEAN

N
W E
S

GREENLAND
(Denmark)

Baffin
Bay

ALASKA
U.S.A.
Anchorage

Nuuk
(Godthåb)

Iqaluit

Largest country
Canada 10 million sq km

Great Bear
Lake

Great Slave
Lake

Hudson
Bay

C A N A D A

St John's

Edmonton

Vancouver   Calgary   Quebec
                                           Montreal   Halifax
Seattle   Winnipeg   Lake   Ottawa
                             Huron
Portland   Lake   Toronto Lake
                        Superior   Ontario   Boston

PACIFIC   Minneapolis   Lake   New York   ATLANTIC
                              Michigan   Detroit Lake
                        Chicago   Erie   OCEAN
OCEAN   Pittsburgh Washington D.C.

Sacramento   Salt Lake   Kansas   St Louis
San   City   Denver   City   Bermuda
Francisco   (UK)
          U N I T E D   S T A T E S

          O F   A M E R I C A

Los Angeles   Atlanta   Country with most people
San Diego   Phoenix   USA 322 million
                            Dallas
              El Paso
                      Houston
                              New Orleans Miami   THE
                                                      BAHAMAS   ANTIGUA AND
                                                                   BARBUDA
                                              Nassau
                                                    DOMINICAN
                        Gulf of   Havana REPUBLIC PUERTO DOMINICA
              Monterrey Mexico   CUBA   RICO   ST LUCIA
                                                   HAITI Santo (USA) BARBADOS
                                                   Port-au- Domingo
                                          JAMAICA Prince   GRENADA
                                          Kingston
MEXICO   Caribbean Sea
Guadalajara
                                        Belmopan
    Mexico City   Puebla   BELIZE
                                        HONDURAS
                        GUATEMALA   Tegucigalpa
                        Guatemala City   SOUTH
                        San Salvador   NICARAGUA
Largest city   EL SALVADOR Managua Panama City AMERICA
Mexico City 22 million   San José PANAMA
                               COSTA RICA

The British Isles
at the same scale.

Manhattan, at the heart of New York, is a centre for business and entertainment.

The U.S. Congress meets in the Capitol building, Washington D.C.

0   400   800   1200   1600   2000 km

Scale : One centimetre on this map is the same as 400 kilometres on the ground.

Total area of North America
25 million sq km

N W E S

ARCTIC OCEAN

EUROPE

Iceland

Greenland

Baffin Bay

Davis Strait

Largest island
Greenland 2 million sq km

Cape Farewell

Ellesmere Island

▲ *Denali 6190*

R. Yukon

Victoria Island

Baffin Island

▲ *Mount Logan 5959*

Gulf of Alaska

R. Mackenzie

Great Bear Lake

Great Slave Lake

Largest lake
Lake Superior 82 100 sq km

Highest mountain
Denali 6190 m

R. Peace

Labrador

Newfoundland

Hudson Bay

Coast Mountains

Rocky Mountains

Great Plains

3954 ▲

Canadian Shield

PACIFIC OCEAN

R. St Lawrence

Lake Superior

Great Lakes

Lake Huron *Lake Ontario* *Cape Cod*

Niagara Falls

ATLANTIC OCEAN

Lake Michigan

Lake Erie

Appalachian Mountains

R. Snake

Great Salt Lake

R. Missouri

R. North Platte

Mount Elbert 4398 ▲

R. Ohio

▲ *2037*

Longest river
Mississippi-Missouri 5969 km

Great Basin

Mount Whitney 4418 ▲

R. Colorado

Grand Canyon

R. Mississippi

R. Red

R. Brazos

Gulf of California

Rio Grande

Sierra Madre Occidental

Sierra Madre Oriental

Florida

Gulf of Mexico

Cuba

Hispaniola

Caribbean Sea

Yucatán

Popocatépetl 5452 ▲

Lake Nicaragua

Isthmus of Panama

SOUTH AMERICA

Key to symbols

🗺 Lake

🗺 Seasonal lake

〜 River

▢ Polar ice cap

Denali 6190 ▲ Mountain and height in metres

Land height above sea level in metres

over 5000
2000 – 5000
1000 – 2000
500 – 1000
200 – 500
0 – 200

The Grand Canyon, a wide, deep gorge in the southwest of the USA.

The Niagara Falls, a set of massive waterfalls in Canada and the USA.

0   400   800   1200   1600   2000 km

Scale : One centimetre on this map is the same as 400 kilometres on the ground.

3

A · B · C · D · E · F

170° W · 4 · 160° W · 5 · 150° W · 140° W · 120° W

60° N · 70° N · 80° N

Arctic Circle

Point Hope
Point Barrow
Barrow
Prudhoe Bay

Beaufort Sea

Brooks Range

Prince Patrick Island

P a r r y
Melville Island

Banks Island

Stefansson Island

Aleutian Islands

Platinum

Nome
Seward Peninsula
St Lawrence Island

U.S.A.

A L A S K A

Alaska Range

Fairbanks

Fort Yukon

R. Yukon

Inuvik

Fort McPherson

Fort Good Hope

R. Arctic Red
R. Mackenzie

Great Bear Lake

Victoria Island

Bathurst Inlet

N

R. Back

50° N

Kodiak Island
Kodiak
Kenai
Seward
Anchorage
Glennallen

Gulf of Alaska

Denali 6190 ▲

Mount Logan 5959 ▲

Dawson

Y U K O N

Whitehorse

R. Yukon

Mackenzie Mountains

N O R T H W E S T

R. Liard

R. Taltson

R. Back

R. Liard

Watson Lake

Yellowknife
Great Slave Lake
Reliance

T E R R I T O R I E S

C

Skagway
Mount Fairweather 4670 ▲
Juneau

Alexander Archipelago

Ketchikan

C
o
a
s
t

M
o
u
n
t
a
i
n
s

R. Stikine

Stewart

Fort Nelson

Mount Lloyd George 2972 ▲

Hay River

R. Taltson

Uranium City

Fort Chipewyan

Lake Athabasca

O C E A N

A

2

PACIFIC

OCEAN

Haida Gwaii (Queen Charlotte Islands)

Prince Rupert

Kitimat

Ocean Falls

Mount Waddington 4042 ▲

BRITISH

COLUMBIA

Dawson Creek

Prince George

Mount Robson 3954 ▲

R. Fraser

R. Peace

Peace River

R. Peace

Grande Prairie

Slave Lake

R. Slave

La Ronge

R. Churchill

Reindeer Lake

Thompson

M A N

Flin Flon

Campbell River

Vancouver Island

Victoria

Seattle

Olympia

Portland

Key to symbols

◪ Countries
■ Capital city
○ Main city/town
∘ Other city/town
— Road
╫ Railway
〜 Canal
✈ Airport
〰 Lake
〰 Seasonal lake
〜 River
Denali ▲ Mountain and
6190   height in metres

CO. CONNECTICUT
MASS. MASSACHUSETTS
N.H. NEW HAMPSHIRE
P.E.I. PRINCE EDWARD ISLAND
PENN. PENNSYLVANIA
R.I. RHODE ISLAND
VER. VERMONT

Vancouver

Kamloops

Kelowna

Cranbrook

Jasper

Edmonton

A L B E R T A

Lloydminster

Banff

Calgary

Medicine Hat

Lethbridge

Shelby

R. North Saskatchewan

S A S K A T C H E W A N

Prince Albert

Saskatoon

R. South Saskatchewan

Moose Jaw

Regina

Brandon

The Pas

Lake Winnipegosis

Lake Manitoba

Dauphin

Lake Winnipeg

Winnipeg

Mount St Helens 2550 ▲
Mount Rainier 4392 ▲

WASHINGTON

Spokane

R. Columbia

R. Snake

MONTANA

Missoula

Great Falls

R. Missouri

Glasgow

Minot

Grand Forks

Fargo

1

Crescent City

Salem

Eugene

La Grande

OREGON

Boise

Bitterroot Range

Billings

R. Yellowstone

NORTH DAKOTA

Williston

Miles City

Bismarck

R. James

U N I T E D

S

40° N

Klamath Falls

Mount Shasta 4317 ▲

Redding

IDAHO

Idaho Falls

Twin Falls

R. Snake

Buffalo

WYOMING

Gannett Peak 4202 ▲

Casper

SOUTH DAKOTA

Rapid City

Sioux Falls

R. Missouri

CALIFORNIA

Sacramento
San Francisco
Oakland
San Jose

Reno

Carson City

NEVADA

Great Basin

Fresno

Mount Whitney 4418 ▲

R. Humboldt

Great Salt Lake

Salt Lake City

Ely

Mount Wheeler 3982 ▲

Tonopah

UTAH

Green River

COLORADO

Cheyenne

R. North Platte

North Platte

NEBRASKA

R. Green

OF AMER

Omaha

Sioux City

120° W · 110° W · 100° W

F · G · H

0 · 200 · 400 · 600 · 800 km

H I J K L M N O P 5 Q 4

6

80° N
40° W
30° W
20° W
10° W
70° N
60° W

GREENLAND
(Denmark)

Qaanaaq

Cape
Parry

Baffin
Bay

Denmark Strait

Iceland
Seyðisfjörður
Höfn
Ísafjörður
Reykjavík

Arctic Circle

60° N

Devon
Island

Resolute

Somerset
Island

Arctic
Bay

Gulf of
Boothia

Baffin
Island

Clyde River

Saqqaq
Disko

Kong Christian IX Land
Gunnbjørn Field
3700

Ellesmere Island
80° W
60° W

Queen
Elizabeth
Islands
100° W

Boothia
Peninsula

Melville
Peninsula

Prince
Charles
Island

Pangnirtung

Davis Strait

Tasiilaq

3

Repulse Bay

Foxe
Basin

Amadjuak
Lake

Iqaluit

Nuuk
(Godthåb)

Kong Frederick VI Kyst

Cape Farewell

Nanortalik

Labrador   Sea

ATLANTIC

50° N

Qamanittuaq

Southampton
Island
Coral
Harbour

Hudson Strait

Kangiqsujuaq

Salluit

NEWFOUNDLAND

OCEAN

kin Inlet

Coats
Island

Mansel
Island

A V U T

D

Churchill

Hudson

Bay

Belcher
Islands

Inukjuak

Kangiqsualujjuaq
R. George

Kuujjuaq

AND LABRADOR

2

Fort Severn

elson

Reservoir
La Grande 2
Chisasibi

Schefferville

Smallwood
Reservoir

Labrador

R. Churchill

Hopedale

Happy Valley
Goose Bay

Port Hope
Simpson

St Anthony

Sandy Lake

BA

Sioux
Lookout

ora

Fort Frances

SOTA

Duluth

Minneapolis

St Paul

Albert

Green Bay

WISCONSIN

Milwaukee

Cedar
Rapids

Chicago

Des Moines

O N T A R I O

R. Albany
Fort
Albany

Moosonee

R. Moose

Lake
Nipigon
Nipigon

Thunder Bay

Longlac

Chapleau

Lake Superior

Sault
Sainte Marie

Escanaba

Lansing

Detroit

South
Bend

Toledo

Cleveland

Timmins

Val-d'Or

Reservoir
La Grande 3
R. Eastmain

Eastmain

Lac
Caniapiscau

Q U E B E C

Chibougamau

Lac Mistassini

R. Harricana

Chicoutimi

Jonquière

Rivière-du-Loup

Trois-Rivières

R. Ottawa

Sherbrooke

North
Bay

Ottawa

Kingston

Toronto

Hamilton

Buffalo

Lake Ontario

Rochester

Sudbury

Traverse
City

MICHIGAN

Flint

Lake Erie

Erie

NEW YORK

PENN

Allentown

Labrador City

Sept-Îles

Baie-Comeau

St Lawrence

Havre-St-Pierre

Gulf of
St Lawrence

Grand Falls
Windsor

Newfoundland

Channel-Port
aux-Basques

St Pierre
and Miquelon
(France)

Sudney

St John's

Cape Breton
Island

Bathurst

NEW
BRUNSWICK

P.E.I.
Charlottetown

Moncton

Saint
John

NOVA SCOTIA

Halifax

Cape Sable

Québec

Montréal

Mount
Washington
1918

MAINE

N.H.

Augusta

Concord

VT.

MASS

Boston

Providence

Cape Cod

Long Island

New York

Hartford

Oshawa

Lake Michigan

80° W

70° W

60° W

N
W E
S

1

J K L M

PACIFIC OCEAN

CANADA

BRITISH COLUMBIA
ALBERTA
SASKATCHEWAN
MANITOBA

WASHINGTON
Seattle
Olympia
Vancouver Island
Victoria
Vancouver
Kelowna
Cranbrook
Sandpoint
Kalispell
Shelby
Lethbridge
Medicine Hat
Moose Jaw
Regina
Estevan
Glasgow
Swan River
Lake Winnipeg
Lake Manitoba
Dauphin
Brandon
Winnipeg
Grand Forks

MONTANA
Great Falls
Missoula
Helena
Butte
Billings
Miles City
Bismarck
NORTH DAKOTA
Williston
Minot
Fargo

OREGON
Portland
Salem
Eugene
Bend
Burns
La Grande
Richland
Spokane
Ellensburg
Mount Rainier 4392
Mount St Helens 3550
Mount Baker 3285
Cascade Range

IDAHO
Boise
Idaho Falls
Twin Falls

WYOMING
Gannett Peak 4202
Lander
Green River
Rawlins
Casper
Buffalo
Cheyenne

SOUTH DAKOTA
Rapid City
Pierre
Aberdeen
Brookings
Sioux Falls
Sioux City

NEBRASKA
North Platte
Sterling
Omaha
Lincoln

NEVADA
Winnemucca
Elko
Reno
Carson City
Great Basin
Ely
Tonopah
Wheeler Peak 3982

Great Salt Lake
Salt Lake City

UTAH
Richfield
Cedar City
Grand Junction

COLORADO
Denver
Colorado Springs
Burlington
Pueblo
Monte Vista
Trinidad
Wheeler Peak 4011

KANSAS
Kansas City
Junction City
Independence
Dodge City
Wichita
Arkansas City

ROCKY MOUNTAINS

UNITED STATES OF AMERICA

CALIFORNIA
Crescent City
Eureka
Ukiah
Redding
Sacramento
San Francisco
Oakland
San Jose
Salinas
San Luis Obispo
Fresno
Bakersfield
Point Conception
Oxnard
Los Angeles
Riverside
Santa Ana
San Diego
Mount Shasta 4317
Mount Whitney 4418
Death Valley
Sierra Nevada
Coast Ranges
Klamath Falls

ARIZONA
Las Vegas
Needles
Flagstaff
Grand Canyon
Colorado Plateau
Phoenix
Tucson
Yuma
Nogales

NEW MEXICO
Santa Fe
Albuquerque
Clovis
Silver City
Artesia
El Paso
Baldy Peak 3476

OKLAHOMA
Clinton
Oklahoma City
Fort Smith
Tulsa

TEXAS
Amarillo
Lubbock
Wichita Falls
Midland
Pecos
Abilene
Fort Worth
Dallas
Waco
Del Rio
Austin
San Antonio
Houston
Corpus Christi
Laredo
Nuevo Laredo
Matamoros
Reynosa
Galveston
Edwards Plateau
Emory Peak 2389

MEXICO
Tijuana
Mexicali
Ensenada
San Felipe
Picacho del Diablo 3096
Lázaro Cárdenas
Caborca
Hermosillo
Guaymas
Santa Rosalia
Ciudad Obregón
Los Mochis
Culiacán
Guadalupe (Mexico)
Punta Eugenia
Villa Insurgentes
La Paz
Cabo Falso
San José del Cabo
Mazatlán
Durango
Torreón
Saltillo
Monterrey
Monclova
Piedras Negras
Ciudad Juárez
Ojinaga
Chihuahua
Hidalgo del Parral
Jiménez
Cerro Peña Nevada 3644
Ciudad Victoria

Baja California
Gulf of California
Sierra Madre Occidental
Sierra Madre Oriental

R. Columbia
R. Snake
R. Salmon
R. Humboldt
R. Colorado
R. Green
R. Yellowstone
R. Missouri
R. North Platte
R. South Platte
R. Platte
R. Arkansas
R. Kansas
R. Canadian
R. Red
R. Brazos
R. Pecos
R. Colorado
R. Rio Grande
R. Gila
R. Sonora
R. Yaqui
R. Nazas
R. Salado
R. Cheyenne
R. James
R. Souris
R. South Saskatchewan

Tropic of Cancer

125° W, 120° W, 115° W, 110° W, 105° W, 100° W, 95° W
50° N, 45° N, 40° N, 35° N, 30° N, 25° N

PACIFIC OCEAN

N W E S

0 200 400 600 800 km

Scale : One centimetre on this map is the same as 120 kilometres on the ground.

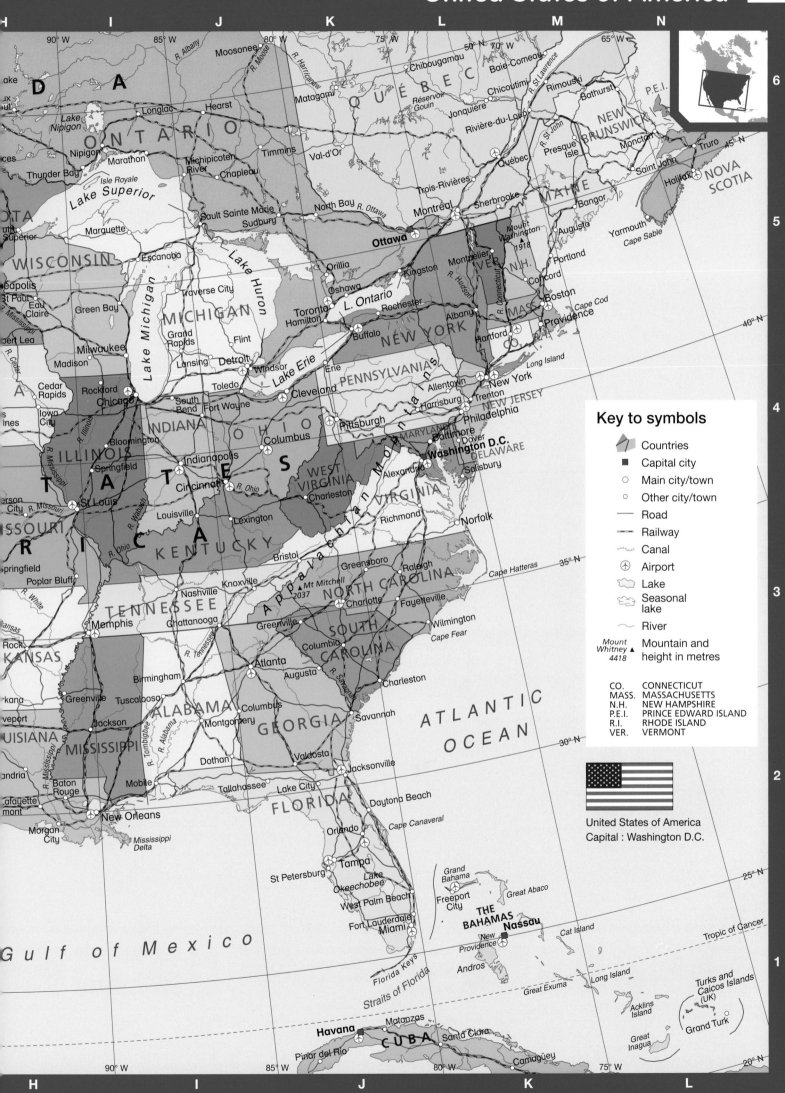

Key to symbols

- ◤ Countries
- ■ Capital city
- ⊙ Main city/town
- ○ Other city/town
- — Road
- ⊣⊢ Railway
- ⌁ Canal
- ✈ Airport
- ⬭ Lake
- ⬰ Seasonal lake
- ∼ River
- *Mount Whitney* ▲ 4418   Mountain and height in metres

CO.	CONNECTICUT
MASS.	MASSACHUSETTS
N.H.	NEW HAMPSHIRE
P.E.I.	PRINCE EDWARD ISLAND
R.I.	RHODE ISLAND
VER.	VERMONT

United States of America
Capital : Washington D.C.

Key to symbols

- Countries
- Capital city
- ○ Main city/town
- ○ Other city/town
- — Road
- Railway
- ▲ Sierra Nevada del Cocuy 5493
- Canal
- Airport
- Lake
- Seasonal lake
- River
- ▲ Mountain and height in metres

Antigua and Barbuda L3
Capital : St John's

The Bahamas I5
Capital : Nassau

Barbados M2
Capital : Bridgetown

Belize G3
Capital : Belmopan

Costa Rica G2
Capital : San José

Cuba H4
Capital : Havana

Dominica L3
Capital : Roseau

Dominican Republic J3
Capital : Santo Domingo

El Salvador G2
Capital : San Salvador

Grenada L2
Capital : St George's

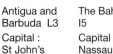

0   200   400   600   800 km

Scale : One centimetre on this map is the same as 135 kilometres on the ground.

H   I   J   K   L   M

85° W   80° W   75° W   70° W   65° W   60° W

ATLANTIC

OCEAN

Greenville
Atlanta
Columbia
Augusta
SOUTH
CAROLINA
Wilmington
Cape Fear
Charleston
Savannah
GEORGIA
Columbus
ontgomery
Valdosta
Jacksonville
Lake City
Tallahassee
FLORIDA
Daytona Beach
Orlando
Cape Canaveral
St Petersburg
Tampa
Lake
Okeechobee
West Palm Beach
Fort Lauderdale
Miami

Bermuda
(UK)
Hamilton

N
W   E
S

30° N
60° W

25° N

Grand
Bahama
Freeport
City
Great Abaco
THE
BAHAMAS
New
Providence
Nassau
Cat Island
Andros
Florida Keys
Straits of Florida
Great Exuma
Long Island

Tropic of Cancer

Havana
Matanzas
Pinar del Río
Guane
Santa Clara
CUBA
Cabo
Antonio
ún
Isla de la
Juventud
Camagüey
Holguín
Bayamo
Guantánamo
Sa Maestra
Santiago
de Cuba
Port-de-Paix
Cap-Haïtien
Acklins
Island
Great
Inagua
Turks and
Caicos Islands
(UK)
Grand Turk
Santiago
Pico Duarte
3175
Hispaniola
San
Juan
Virgin Is
(UK)
Virgin Is
(USA)
Leeward Islands
Anguilla (UK) St-Martin (France)
Sint
Maarten
(Neth.)
Barbuda
ANTIGUA AND
BARBUDA
St John's
Antigua
Guadeloupe
(France)

20° N

Greater
Cayman
Islands
(UK)
Montego Bay
JAMAICA
Kingston
Jérémie
HAITI
Port-au-
Prince
Santo
Domingo
DOMINICAN
REPUBLIC
Ponce
PUERTO
RICO
(USA)
ST KITTS
AND NEVIS
Montserrat
(UK)
DOMINICA
Roseau
Martinique
(France)
Castries
ST LUCIA
Kingstown

15° N

Caribbean
Antilles
Lesser Antilles
Windward Is
BARBADOS
Bridgetown
ST VINCENT AND
THE GRENADINES
GRENADA
St George's

Sea
Lesser Antilles
Punta Gallinas
Aruba
(Neth.)
Curaçao
(Neth.)
Port of Spain
TRINIDAD
& TOBAGO
Tobago
Güiria Trinidad

NICARAGUA
Managua
Lake
aragua
Río Grande
Ríohacha
Coro
Cumaná
Barcelona
Maturín
R. Tigre
10° N

COSTA RICA
San José
Chirripó
3819
Panama Canal
Colón
Isthmus of Panama
David
Aguadulce
Panama City
PANAMA
Turbo
Sincelejo
Montería
Barranquilla
Cartagena
Valledupar
Maracaibo
Barquisimeto
Caracas
Valencia
Maracay
Lake
Maracaibo
Acarigua
El Tigre
Ciudad
Guayana
Orinoco
Delta

COLOMBIA
Cúcuta
San Cristóbal
Barinas
San Fernando
de Apure
Ciudad Bolívar
R. Orinoco
Embalse
de Guri
El Callao

Medellín
Bucaramanga
Sierra Nevada
del Cocuy
5493
R. Meta
Llanos
VENEZUELA
Guiana
Highlands
5° N

85° W   80° W   75° W   70° W   65° W

6

5

4

3

2

1

Caribbean Sea

Total population of South America
418 million

Barranquilla Maracaibo **Caracas** **Port of Spain**
TRINIDAD
AND TOBAGO

NORTH
AMERICA

VENEZUELA **Georgetown**
Paramaribo
Cayenne

Medellín SURINAME
FRENCH
GUIANA

Bogotá
COLOMBIA

Cali

Largest country
Brazil 9 million sq km

ATLANTIC

OCEAN

Quito
ECUADOR

Guayaquil

Galapagos Islands
(Ecuador)

Iquitos

Manaus

Belém

São Luís

Country with most people
Brazil 208 million

Fortaleza

Natal

B R A Z I L

Trujillo

PERU

Lima

Recife

Aracaju

Salvador

PACIFIC

OCEAN

Lake
Titicaca

BOLIVIA
La Paz

Sucre

Arequipa

Brasília

Belo Horizonte

Antofagasta

PARAGUAY
Asunción

São Paulo

Rio de
Janeiro

Largest city
São Paulo 21 million

Curitiba

ATLANTIC

OCEAN

Juan Fernandez Islands
(Chile)

Valparaíso
Santiago

Concepción

Porto Alegre

URUGUAY
Buenos
Aires **Montevideo**

Mar del Plata

Falkland Islands (UK)
Claimed by Argentina

Key to symbols

Countries

■ Capital city

○ Important city/town

Punta
Arenas Tierra
del
Fuego

South Georgia
(UK)

The British Isles
at the same scale.

The statue known as Christ the Redeemer overlooks Rio de Janeiro.

The ruins of the lost Inca city of Machu Picchu in Peru.

0 400 800 1200 1600 2000 km

Scale : One centimetre on this map is the same as 400 kilometres on the ground.

Total area of South America
18 million sq km

Longest river
River Amazon 6516 km

Largest lake
Lake Titicaca 8340 sq km

Highest mountain
Aconcagua 6959 m

Largest island
Tierra del Fuego 47 000 sq km

Caribbean Sea

N
W E
S

ATLANTIC OCEAN

NORTH AMERICA

Llanos
Lake Maracaibo
Orinoco Delta
R. Orinoco
Angel Falls
Mount Roraima 2810
Guiana Highlands
R. Japurá
R. Negro
R. Amazon
Mouths of the Amazon

Galapagos Islands

Amazon Basin
Selvas
R. Amazon
R. Madeira
R. Purus
R. Tocantins
R. São Francisco

PACIFIC OCEAN

Andes
Atacama Desert
Altiplano
Lake Titicaca

Brazilian Highlands

R. Paraguay
Gran Chaco
Nevado Ojos del Salado 6908
R. Salado
R. Paraná
R. Uruguay

ATLANTIC OCEAN

Aconcagua 6959
Pampas
Rio de la Plata

Juan Fernandez Islands

R. Colorado
R. Negro

Andes

Isla de Chiloé
Valdes Peninsula

Patagonia

Falkland Islands

Tierra del Fuego
Cape Horn
South Georgia

Key to symbols

- 🌊 Lake
- 🌊 Seasonal lake
- ～ River
- *Aconcagua* ▲ Mountain and
  6959 height in metres

Land height above sea level in metres

over 5000
2000 – 5000
1000 – 2000
500 – 1000
200 – 500
0 – 200

Wild horses in Patagonia, Chile.

The Amazon rainforest covers more than one third of Brazil.

0   400   800   1200   1600   2000 km

Scale : One centimetre on this map is the same as 400 kilometres on the ground.

ATLANTIC OCEAN

Caribbean Sea

Lesser Antilles

DOMINICA
ST LUCIA
ST VINCENT & THE GRENADINES
GRENADA
BARBADOS
Martinique (France)
TRINIDAD & TOBAGO
Port Of Spain

NICARAGUA
COSTA RICA
PANAMA
Panama City

Barranquilla
Cartagena
Montería
Sincelejo
Aruba (Neth.)
Coro
Maracaibo
Lake Maracaibo
Valencia
Barquisimeto
Caracas
Maracay
Barcelona
Güiria
Maturín
Ciudad Bolívar
R. Orinoco
Ciudad Guayana
Orinoco Delta

VENEZUELA
COLOMBIA
ECUADOR
PERU
BOLIVIA

Bucaramanga
Medellín
Manizales
Cali
Bogotá
Tunja
Villavicencio
Florencia
San Cristóbal
Acarigua
Barinas
R. Meta
R. Guaviare
Cordillera Oriental
Cordillera Central
Cordillera Occidental
Llanos Orientales

Pasto
Quito
Cotopaxi 5896
Ambato
Portoviejo
Guayaquil
Machala
Piura
Chiclayo
Trujillo
Chimbote
Huascarán 6768
Huaraz
Lima
Ayacucho
Cusco
Coropuna 6425
Arequipa
Arica
Iquique

Cordillera Central
R. Marañón
Cordillera Occidental
Cordillera Oriental
Altiplano
Cord. Occidental
Sajama 6542
Lake Titicaca
Juliaca
Puno
La Paz
Cochabamba
Sucre
Potosí
Tarija
Santa Cruz
Trinidad
R. Beni
R. Mamoré
R. Guaporé
R. San Miguel

Georgetown
Paramaribo
Cayenne
GUYANA
SURINAME
FRENCH GUIANA
R. Essequibo
Mount Roraima 2810
Boa Vista
R. Branco
Guiana Highlands
Pico da Neblina 3014
R. Negro
R. Orinoco

Mouths of the Amazon
Ilha de Marajó
Belém
Macapá
Manaus
Manacapuru
Balbina Resr.
R. Japurá
R. Caquetá
R. Putumayo
R. Napo
R. Marañón
R. Ucayali
R. Juruá
R. Purus
R. Madre de Dios
R. Madeira
R. Amazon

Amazon Basin
Selvas

BRAZIL

Fortaleza
Natal
Recife
Maceió
Aracaju
Salvador
Caruarú
Garanhuns
Paulo Afonso
Feira de Santana
Itabuna
Parnaíba
Sobral
Teresina
Bragança
São Luís
Bacabal
Imperatriz
Marabá
Tucuruí Resr.
Altamira
Itaituba
R. Xingu
R. Iriri
R. Tapajós
R. Teles Pires
R. Juruena
R. Theodore Roosevelt
R. Aripuanã
R. Jiparaná
R. Tocantins
R. Araguaia

Petrolina
R. São Francisco
Sobradinho Dam
Montes Claros
Luziânia
Brasília
Anápolis
Goiânia
Rio Verde
Rondonópolis
Cuiabá
Campo Grande
Dourados
Corumbá
Cáceres
R. Paraguai
R. Taquari
Chaco

Serra da Mesa Resr.
Brazilian Highlands
Teófilo Otoni
Itambé 2033
Governador Valadares
Linhares
Vitória
Belo Horizonte
Uberaba
Uberlândia
Araguari
Barretos
Barbacena
Aragarças
Filadélfia
Tajfil

Porto Velho
Ariquemes
Rio Branco
Cruzeiro do Sul
Pucallpa

N
W E
S

40°W
50°W
60°W
70°W
80°W
10°N
0° Equator
10°S
20°S

0 200 400 600 800 km

Scale : One centimetre on this map is the same as 200 kilometres on the ground.

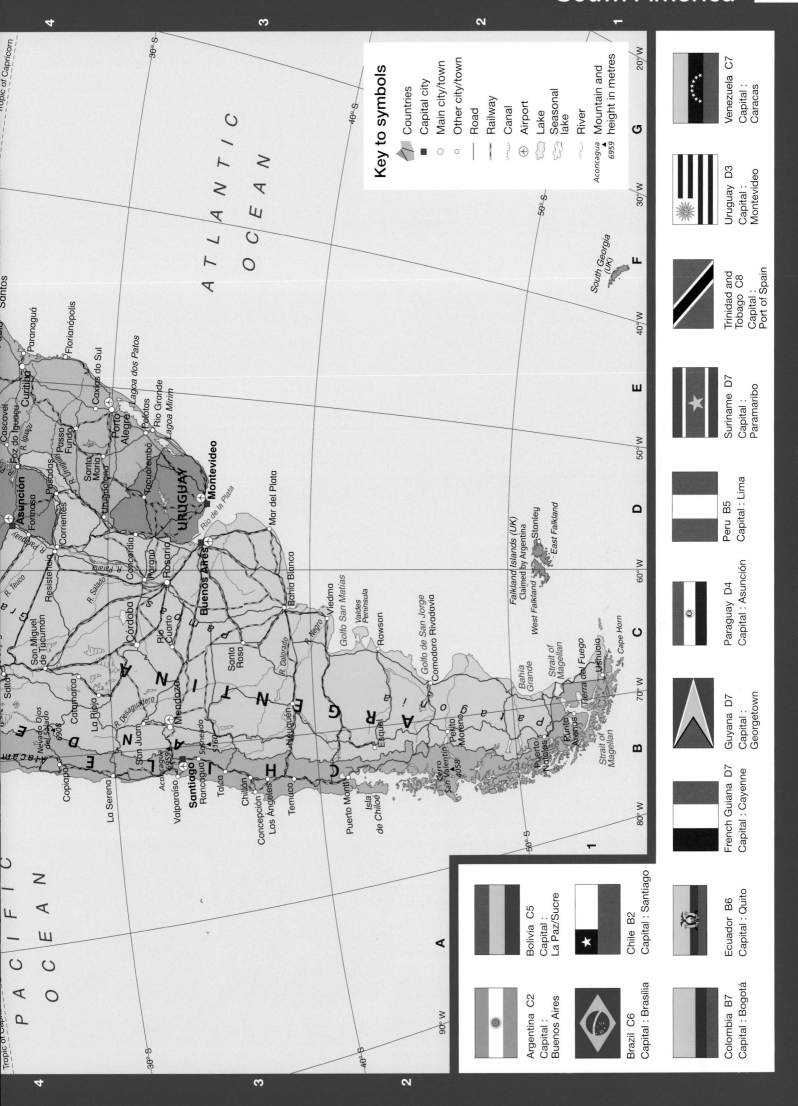

Key to symbols

	Countries	
■	Capital city	
○	Main city/town	
○	Other city/town	
	Road	
	Railway	
	Canal	
✈	Airport	
	Lake	
	Seasonal lake	
	River	
▲ Aconcagua 6959	Mountain and height in metres	

Argentina C2
Capital :
Buenos Aires

Bolivia C5
Capital :
La Paz/Sucre

Brazil C6
Capital : Brasília

Chile B2
Capital : Santiago

Colombia B7
Capital : Bogotá

Ecuador B6
Capital : Quito

French Guiana D7
Capital : Cayenne

Guyana D7
Capital :
Georgetown

Paraguay D4
Capital : Asunción

Peru B5
Capital : Lima

Suriname D7
Capital :
Paramaribo

Trinidad and Tobago C8
Capital :
Port of Spain

Uruguay D3
Capital :
Montevideo

Venezuela C7
Capital :
Caracas

Total population of Oceania
39 million

Key to symbols
- Countries
- ■ Capital city
- ○ Important city/town

N
W E
S

■Yaren
NAURU ·

KIRIBATI

A S I A

New Guinea

Jayapura

Lae

PAPUA NEW GUINEA

SOLOMON ISLANDS

TUVALU

■Honiara

Arafura Sea

■Port Moresby

Timor Sea

○Darwin

Coral Sea

VANUATU

INDIAN

○Cairns

■Port Vila

OCEAN

○Townsville

New Caledonia (France)

FIJI ■Suva

○Rockhampton

■Nouméa

A U S T R A L I A

○Alice Springs

Largest country
Australia 8 million sq km

○Brisbane
○Gold Coast

P A C I F I C

Kati Thanda-Lake Eyre

O C E A N

○Kalgoorlie

○Newcastle
○Sydney

Country with most people
Australia 24 million

Great Australian Bight

○Perth

○Adelaide

■Canberra

Tasman Sea

○Melbourne

○Auckland

○Geelong

North Island

Tasmania

NEW ZEALAND

○Hobart

■Wellington

Largest city
Sydney 5 million

○Christchurch
South Island
○Dunedin

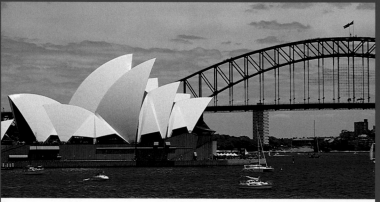
The harbour, bridge and opera house in Sydney, Australia's largest city.

The British Isles at the same scale.

Solomon Islanders perform a traditional dance to entertain tourists.

0 300 600 900 1200 1500 km

Scale : One centimetre on this map is the same as 325 kilometres on the ground.

Key to symbols

⬚ Lake
⬚ Seasonal lake
〰 River
Puncak Jaya ▲ 4884　Mountain and height in metres

Land height above sea level in metres

over 5000
2000 – 5000
1000 – 2000
500 – 1000
200 – 500
0 – 200

⬚ Land below sea level

N
W　E
S

Highest mountain
Puncak Jaya 4884 m

Puncak Jaya ▲ 4884

Mount Wilhelm 4509 ▲

New Guinea

New Ireland

New Britain

Solomon Islands

Largest island
New Guinea 808 510 sq km

Arafura Sea

Timor Sea

Cape York Peninsula

Arnhem Land

Gulf of Carpentaria

Great Barrier Reef

Coral Sea

INDIAN

OCEAN

Kimberley Plateau

R. Fitzroy

Great Sandy Desert

R. Fortescue

Macdonnell Ranges

A u s t r a l i a

Great Dividing Range

863 ▲ *Uluru (Ayers Rock)*

Musgrave Ranges

Great Victoria Desert

Kati Thanda-Lake Eyre

Lake Torrens

Nullarbor Plain

Great Australian Bight

R. Murray

R. Darling
R. Macquarie
R. Lachlan
R. Murrumbidgee
R. Murray

Mount Kosciuszko ▲ 2229

Largest lake
Kati Thanda-Lake Eyre 0–8900 sq km

P A C I F I C

O C E A N

New Caledonia

Fiji

Cape Leeuwin

Longest river
Murray-Darling 3672 km

T a s m a n　S e a

Tasmania

North Cape

North Island

New Zealand

Aoraki / Mount Cook ▲ 3724

South Island

Total area of Oceania
9 million sq km

A diver feeds fish on the Great Barrier Reef, Australia.

Aoraki / Mount Cook, the highest mountain in New Zealand.

0　300　600　900　1200　1500 km
Scale : One centimetre on this map is the same as 325 kilometres on the ground.

A B C D E

Equator 0° 130° E 140° E 150° E

Kepulauan Sula

Seram
Ceram Sea
Doberai Peninsula Manokwari
Jayapura

Buru Ambon

120° E
Buton
Makassar

Kepulauan Kai
Kepulauan Aru

Pegunungan Maoke
▲ 4884 Puncak Jaya

New
Guinea

Admiralty Islands
Bismarck Sea
New Ireland

P A P U A
Mt Wilhelm ▲ 4509
Lae
New Britain

N E W

G U I N E A

Bougainville Island

Solomon Sea

6

Banda Sea

I N D O N E S I A

R. Fly
Kerema
Gulf of Papua
Port Moresby
D'Entrecasteaux Islands

Kepulauan Tanimbar

Tanjung Vals

Wetar
Alor
Flores Sea
Maumere
Flores Flores
Dili
EAST
TIMOR
Kepulauan Leti

EAST TIMOR

Timor

Arafura Sea

Torres Strait

Cape York

Sumbawa
Savu Sea
Kupang

10° S
Sumba

Melville Island

Timor Sea

Darwin
Arnhem Land
R. Daly
Katherine

Groote Eylandt
Gulf of Carpentaria

Wellesley Islands

Cape York Peninsula

Coral Se

R. Mitchell
Great Barrier Reef
Cairns

R. Victoria

5

Kimberley Plateau

Broome

Halls Creek

N O R T H E R N

Barkly Tableland

R. Flinders

Townsville

Mackay

Mount Isa

Tanami Desert

T E R R I T O R Y

Q U E E N S L A N D

Great Dividing Range

Rockhampton

20° S
Port Hedland
Great Sandy Desert

R. Fortescue
Pilbara
Newman

W E S T E R N

Lake Mackay

Lake Disappointment

Mount Zeil 1531
Macdonnell Ranges
Alice Springs

Barcaldine

R. Diamantina

Cooper Creek

Maryborough

Tropic of Capricorn

R. Murchison

Uluru (Ayers Rock) 863
Gibson Desert

A U S T R A L I A

Simpson Desert

R. Warrego

Brisbane
Toowoomba
Gold Coast

Geraldton

A U S T R A L I A

Musgrave Ranges

S O U T H

Kati Thanda-Lake Eyre (North)

Dirranbandi

Grafton

4

Great Victoria Desert

Kati Thanda-Lake Eyre (South)

A U S T R A L I A

Bourke

R. Darling

N E W

S O U T H

Tamworth

Port Macquari

Kalgoorlie
Nullarbor Plain

Lake Gairdner

Lake Torrens

W A L E S

Dubbo

30° S
Geraldton

Norseman

Great Australian Bight

Port Augusta

Broken Hill

R. Lachlan

Bathurst
Newcastle
Sydney

Perth
Fremantle

Esperance

Port Lincoln

Adelaide
Murray Bridge

Hay
R. Murrumbidgee
Wagga Wagga
R. Murray

Wollongong

Canberra
AUST. CAP. TER.

Albany

Cape Leeuwin

Kangaroo Island

Horsham

Mount Gambier

V I C T O R I A

R. Murray

Melbourne

Geelong

▲ Mount Kosciuszko 2229

Great Dividing Range

Bairnsdale

Tas

3

Bass Strait

Burnie

▲ Mount Ossa 1617

TASMANIA

Hobart
South East Cape

Key to symbols

◢ Countries
■ Capital city
○ Main city/town
○ Other city/town
— Road
— Railway

✈ Airport
〰 Lake
〰 Seasonal lake
~ River
Puncak Jaya ▲ 4884 Mountain and height in metres

2

110° E 120° E 130° E 50° S 140° E 150° E

A B C D E

0 200 400 600 800 km

Scale : One centimetre on this map is the same as 200 kilometres on the ground.

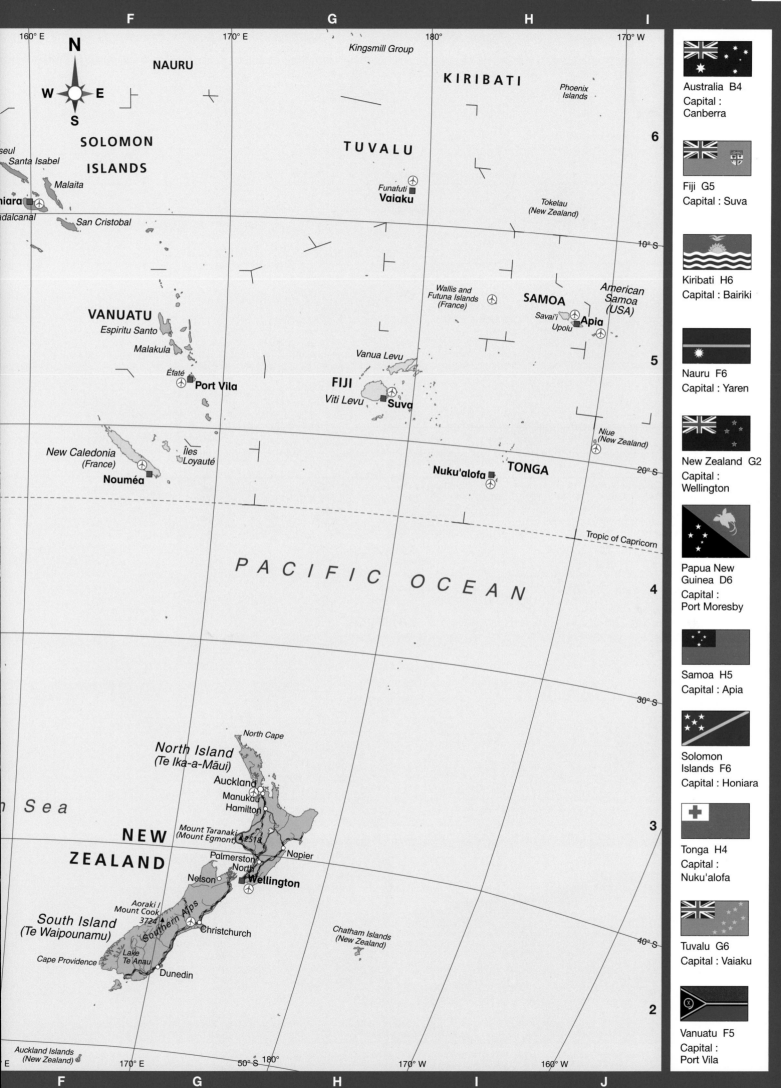

F   G   H   I

160° E   170° E   180°   170° W

N
W · E
S

NAURU

KIRIBATI

Kingsmill Group

Phoenix
Islands

SOLOMON

TUVALU

6

ISLANDS

seul
Santa Isabel

Malaita

niara

adalcanal

San Cristobal

Funafuti
Vaiaku

Tokelau
(New Zealand)

10° S

VANUATU

Espiritu Santo

Malakula

Éfaté
Port Vila

Wallis and
Futuna Islands
(France)

SAMOA

Savai'i
Upolu

Apia

American
Samoa
(USA)

Vanua Levu

FIJI

Viti Levu
Suva

5

New Caledonia
(France)

Îles
Loyauté

Niue
(New Zealand)

Nouméa

Nuku'alofa

TONGA

20° S

Tropic of Capricorn

P A C I F I C   O C E A N

4

30° S

North Cape

North Island
(Te Ika-a-Māui)

Auckland

Manukau

Hamilton

3

Mount Taranaki
(Mount Egmont) ▲2518

NEW

Napier

ZEALAND

Palmerston
North

Nelson

Wellington

Chatham Islands
(New Zealand)

40° S

Aoraki /
Mount Cook
3724 ▲

Southern Alps

South Island
(Te Waipounamu)

Christchurch

Cape Providence

Lake
Te Anau

Dunedin

2

Auckland Islands
(New Zealand)

170° E   50° S 180°   170° W   160° W

F   G   H   I   J

Sea

n Sea

Flags

Australia B4
Capital :
Canberra

Fiji G5
Capital : Suva

Kiribati H6
Capital : Bairiki

Nauru F6
Capital : Yaren

New Zealand G2
Capital :
Wellington

Papua New
Guinea D6
Capital :
Port Moresby

Samoa H5
Capital : Apia

Solomon
Islands F6
Capital : Honiara

Tonga H4
Capital :
Nuku'alofa

Tuvalu G6
Capital : Vaiaku

Vanuatu F5
Capital :
Port Vila

Azores
(Portugal)

EUROPE

N
W · E
S

Total population of Africa
1186 million

Key to symbols
Countries
Capital city
Important city/town

ASIA

Largest country
Algeria 2 million sq km

Mediterranean Sea

Algiers

Madeira
(Portugal)

Rabat
Casablanca

Tunis
TUNISIA

Tripoli

Alexandria
Giza · Cairo

Canary Is
(Spain)

MOROCCO

ALGERIA

LIBYA

Benghazi

EGYPT

Laayoune

Red Sea

WESTERN
SAHARA

MAURITANIA

Nouakchott

MALI

NIGER

CHAD

SUDAN

ERITREA
Asmara

Khartoum

DJIBOUTI
Djibouti

CAPE VERDE

Praia

Dakar
SENEGAL
THE
GAMBIA
GUINEA-
BISSAU

Banjul

Bissau

Bamako
BURKINA FASO
Ouagadougou

Niamey

Lake Chad
Ndjamena

Addis
Ababa

ETHIOPIA

Conakry
Freetown

GUINEA
SIERRA
LEONE

CÔTE
D'IVOIRE
Yamoussoukro

GHANA Porto-
Novo

NIGERIA
Abuja

CENTRAL
AFRICAN
REPUBLIC

SOUTH
SUDAN

Juba

Lake
Turkana

SOMALIA

Mogadishu

Monrovia
LIBERIA

Accra

Lagos

Lomé

CAMEROON

Bangui

UGANDA KENYA

Kampala

INDIAN

Abidjan

Largest city
Lagos 13 million

Malabo
EQUATORIAL
GUINEA

Yaoundé

DEMOCRATIC

RWANDA
Kigali
BURUNDI

Nairobi

OCEAN

Country with most people
Nigeria 182 million

São
Tomé
SÃO TOMÉ
& PRÍNCIPE

Libreville

GABON

CONGO

REPUBLIC

OF THE

Brazzaville

Kinshasa

CONGO

Lake
Victoria

SEYCHELLES

Lake
Tanganyika

Bujumbura

Dodoma

TANZANIA

Mombasa

Victoria

Dar es Salaam

Aldabra Is
(Seychelles)

Ascension
Island
(UK)

Luanda

ATLANTIC

St Helena (UK)

ANGOLA

Moroni
COMOROS

Mayotte
(France)

Lilongwe

Lake
Nyasa

OCEAN

ZAMBIA

Lusaka

MALAWI

MOZAMBIQUE

MADAGASCAR

Antananarivo

MAURITIUS

NAMIBIA

Windhoek

Harare

ZIMBABWE

Beira

Reunion
(France)

Port
Louis

Walvis Bay

BOTSWANA

Gaborone

Pretoria

Maputo

Johannesburg

SWAZILAND

Mbabane

Maseru

SOUTH

Bloemfontein

LESOTHO

AFRICA

Cape Town

The British Isles
at the same scale.

Cape Town, South Africa.

The giant pyramids at Giza, Egypt.

0   450   900   1350   1800   2250 km

Scale : One centimetre on this map is the same as 450 kilometres on the ground.

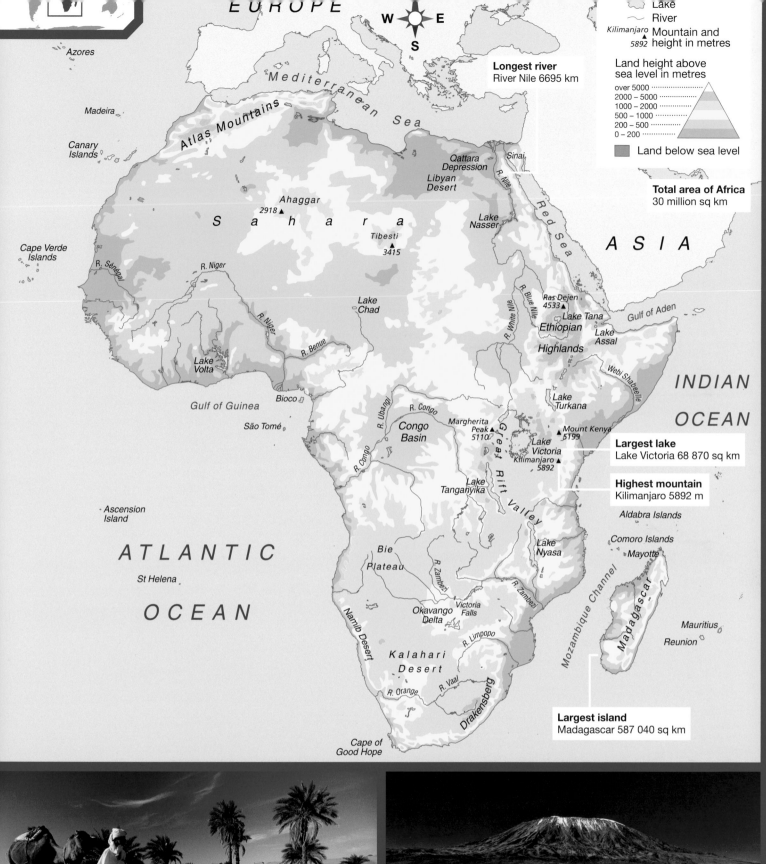

EUROPE

W N E S

Azores

Madeira

Canary
Islands

Cape Verde
Islands

Mediterranean Sea

Atlas Mountains

S a h a r a

Ahaggar
2918 ▲

Tibesti
▲
3415

R. Sénégal

R. Niger

R. Niger

R. Benue

Lake
Chad

Lake
Volta

Bioco

Gulf of Guinea

São Tomé

R. Ubangi

R. Congo

Congo
Basin

R. Congo

ATLANTIC

· Ascension
Island

St Helena ·

OCEAN

Namib Desert

Bie
Plateau

R. Zambezi

Okavango
Delta

Victoria
Falls

R. Zambezi

K a l a h a r i
D e s e r t

R. Orange

R. Vaal

R. Limpopo

Drakensberg

Cape of
Good Hope

Qattara
Depression
Libyan
Desert

Sinai

R. Nile

Lake
Nasser

Red Sea

ASIA

Gulf of Aden

R. Blue Nile

Ras Dejen
4533 ▲

Lake Tana

Ethiopian
Highlands

Lake
Assal

R. White Nile

Webi Shabeelle

Lake
Turkana

Margherita
Peak ▲
5110

Great Rift Valley

Mount Kenya
▲ 5199

Lake
Victoria

Kilimanjaro ▲
5892

Lake
Tanganyika

Lake
Nyasa

INDIAN

OCEAN

Aldabra Islands

Comoro Islands

Mayotte

Mozambique Channel

Madagascar

Mauritius

Reunion

Longest river
River Nile 6695 km

▬ Lake
〰 River
Kilimanjaro ▲ Mountain and
5892 height in metres

Land height above
sea level in metres
over 5000 ·············
2000 – 5000 ·············
1000 – 2000 ·············
500 – 1000 ·············
200 – 500 ·············
0 – 200 ·············

☐ Land below sea level

Total area of Africa
30 million sq km

Largest lake
Lake Victoria 68 870 sq km

Highest mountain
Kilimanjaro 5892 m

Largest island
Madagascar 587 040 sq km

A Bedouin nomad in the Sahara Desert with his camels.

Kilimanjaro, an extinct volcano, is the highest mountain in Africa.

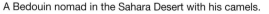

0   450   900   1350   1800   2250 km

Scale : One centimetre on this map is the same as 450 kilometres on the ground.

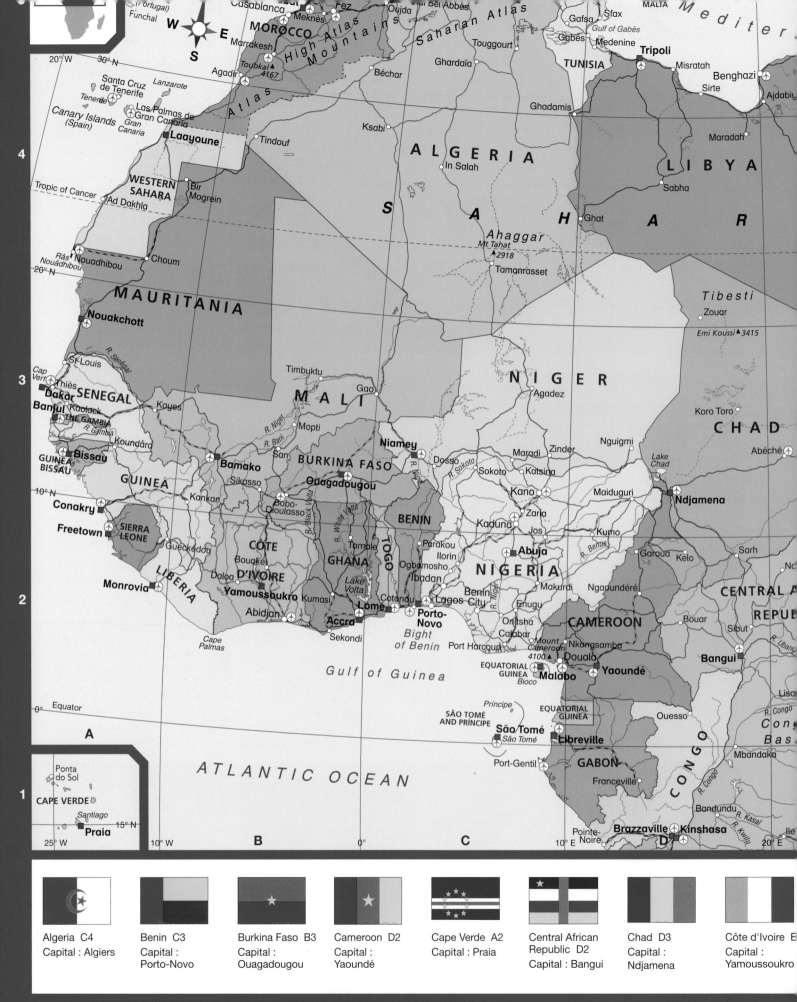

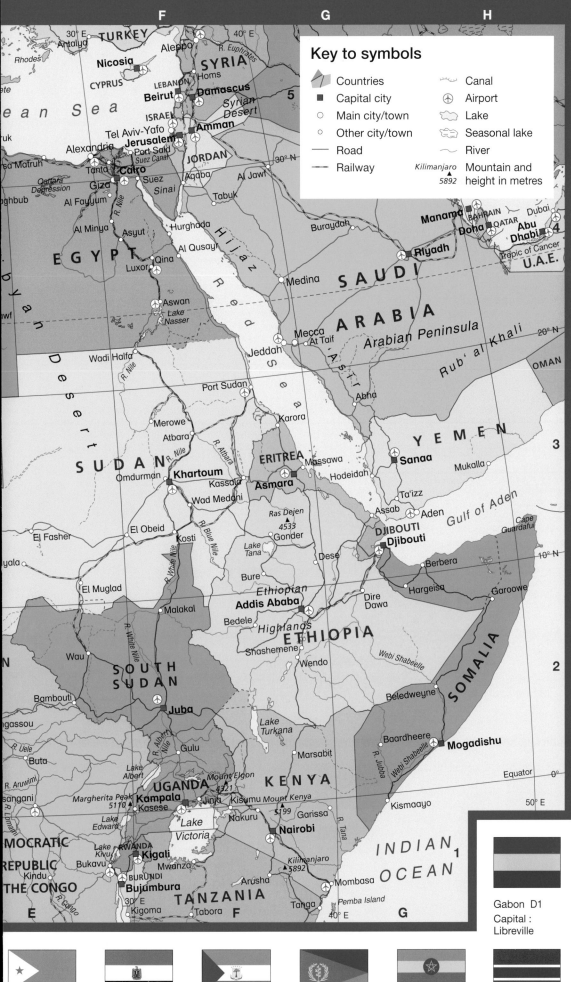

Key to symbols

◢ Countries	〰 Canal
■ Capital city	✈ Airport
○ Main city/town	🝆 Lake
○ Other city/town	🝆 Seasonal lake
— Road	〜 River
— Railway	Kilimanjaro ▲ 5892 Mountain and height in metres

Selected map labels:

TURKEY, Antalya, Rhodes, Nicosia, CYPRUS, Aleppo, R. Euphrates, SYRIA, Homs, Beirut, LEBANON, Damascus, ISRAEL, Tel Aviv-Yafo, Jerusalem, Amman, JORDAN, Syrian Desert, Aqaba, Al Jawf, Tabuk, Mediterranean Sea, Alexandria, Port Said, Suez Canal, Cairo, Giza, Suez, Sinai, Al Fayyum, Qattara Depression, Siwa, Matruh, EGYPT, Al Minya, Asyut, Qina, Luxor, Aswan, Hurghada, Al Qusayr, Lake Nasser, Wadi Halfa, R. Nile, Hijaz, Medina, Mecca, At Taif, Jeddah, SAUDI ARABIA, Buraydah, Riyadh, Manama, BAHRAIN, Doha, QATAR, Abu Dhabi, U.A.E., Dubai, Tropic of Cancer, Arabian Peninsula, Rub' al Khali, OMAN, Port Sudan, Karora, Merowe, Atbara, Omdurman, Khartoum, Kassala, Wad Medani, SUDAN, R. Atbara, El Obeid, Kosti, El Fasher, ERITREA, Massawa, Asmara, Hodeidah, YEMEN, Sanaa, Mukalla, Ta'izz, Abha, 'Asir, Red Sea, Ras Dejen 4533, Gonder, Lake Tana, Dese, Bure, El Muglad, R. Blue Nile, R. White Nile, Malakal, Bedele, Addis Ababa, ETHIOPIA, Ethiopian Highlands, Shashemene, Wendo, Assab, Aden, Gulf of Aden, DJIBOUTI, Djibouti, Berbera, Hargeisa, Garoowe, Cape Guardafui, Webi Shabeelle, SOMALIA, Beledweyne, Baardheere, Mogadishu, Wau, SOUTH SUDAN, Juba, Bambouti, Gulu, R. Albert Nile, Lake Albert, Lake Turkana, Marsabit, KENYA, R. Jubba, Kismaayo, Bukavu, Kindu, DEMOCRATIC REPUBLIC OF THE CONGO, Lake Kivu, RWANDA, Kigali, BURUNDI, Bujumbura, Mwanza, Kigoma, Tabora, TANZANIA, Arusha, Kilimanjaro 5892, Mombasa, Pemba Island, Tanga, INDIAN OCEAN, Equator, UGANDA, Kampala, Margherita Peak 5170, Kasese, Lake Edward, Mount Elgon 4321, Jinja, Lake Victoria, Kisumu, Mount Kenya 5199, Nakuru, Nairobi, Garissa, R. Tana

Flag legend:

 Ghana B2 Capital : Accra

 São Tomé and Príncipe C2 Capital : São Tomé

 Guinea A3 Capital : Conakry

 Senegal A3 Capital : Dakar

 Guinea-Bissau A3 Capital : Bissau

 Sierra Leone A2 Capital : Freetown

 Liberia A2 Capital : Monrovia

 Somalia G2 Capital : Mogadishu

 Libya D4 Capital : Tripoli

 South Sudan E2 Capital : Juba

 Mali B3 Capital : Bamako

 Sudan E3 Capital : Khartoum

 Mauritania A3 Capital : Nouakchott

 Togo C2 Capital : Lomé

 Morocco B5 Capital : Rabat

 Tunisia C5 Capital : Tunis

 Gabon D1 Capital : Libreville

 Niger C3 Capital : Niamey

 Uganda F2 Capital : Kampala

 Djibouti G3 Capital : Djibouti

 Egypt E4 Capital : Cairo

 Equatorial Guinea C2 Capital : Malabo

 Eritrea F3 Capital : Asmara

 Ethiopia F2 Capital : Addis Ababa

 The Gambia A3 Capital : Banjul

Nigeria C2 Capital : Abuja

Western Sahara A4 Capital : Laayoune

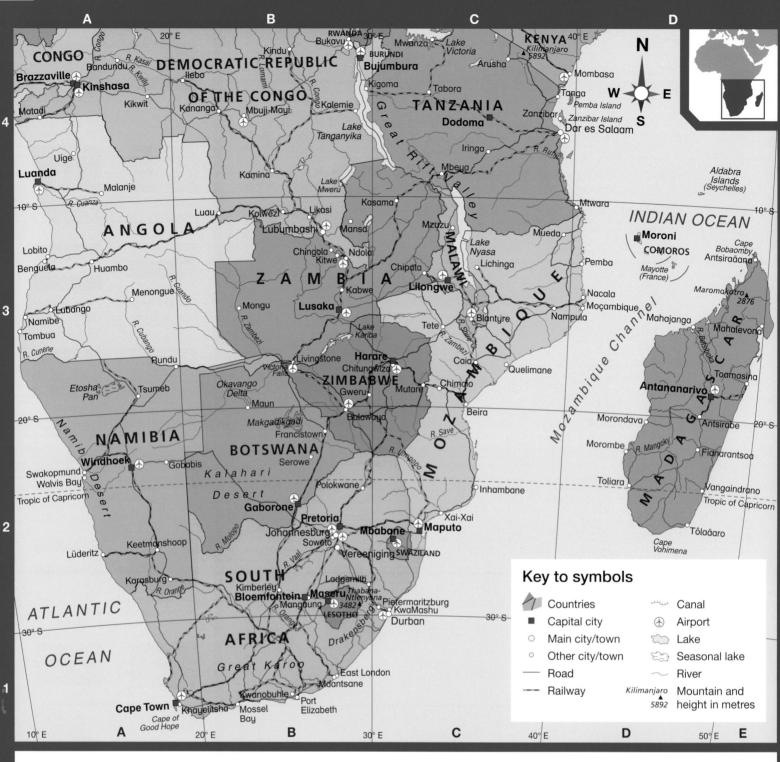

N
W E
S

Key to symbols

	Countries		Canal
■	Capital city	⊕	Airport
○	Main city/town		Lake
∘	Other city/town		Seasonal lake
—	Road	～	River
╪	Railway	▲ Kilimanjaro 5892	Mountain and height in metres

0 200 400 600 800 km

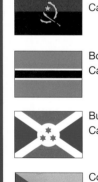 Angola A3
Capital : Luanda

 Botswana B2
Capital : Gaborone

 Burundi B4
Capital : Bujumbura

Comoros D3
Capital : Moroni

Congo A4
Capital : Brazzaville

 Democratic Republic
of the Congo B4
Capital : Kinshasa

 Kenya C4
Capital : Nairobi

 Lesotho B2
Capital : Maseru

Madagascar D2
Capital :
Antananarivo

 Malawi C3
Capital : Lilongwe

 Mauritius *see page 54*
Capital : Port Louis

 Mozambique C2
Capital : Maputo

 Namibia A2
Capital : Windhoek

 Rwanda B4
Capital : Kigali

 Seychelles *see page 54*
Capital : Victoria

 South Africa B2
Capital :
Pretoria/Cape Town/
Bloemfontein

 Swaziland C2
Capital : Mbabane

 Tanzania C4
Capital : Dodoma

 Zambia B3
Capital : Lusaka

 Zimbabwe B3
Capital : Harare

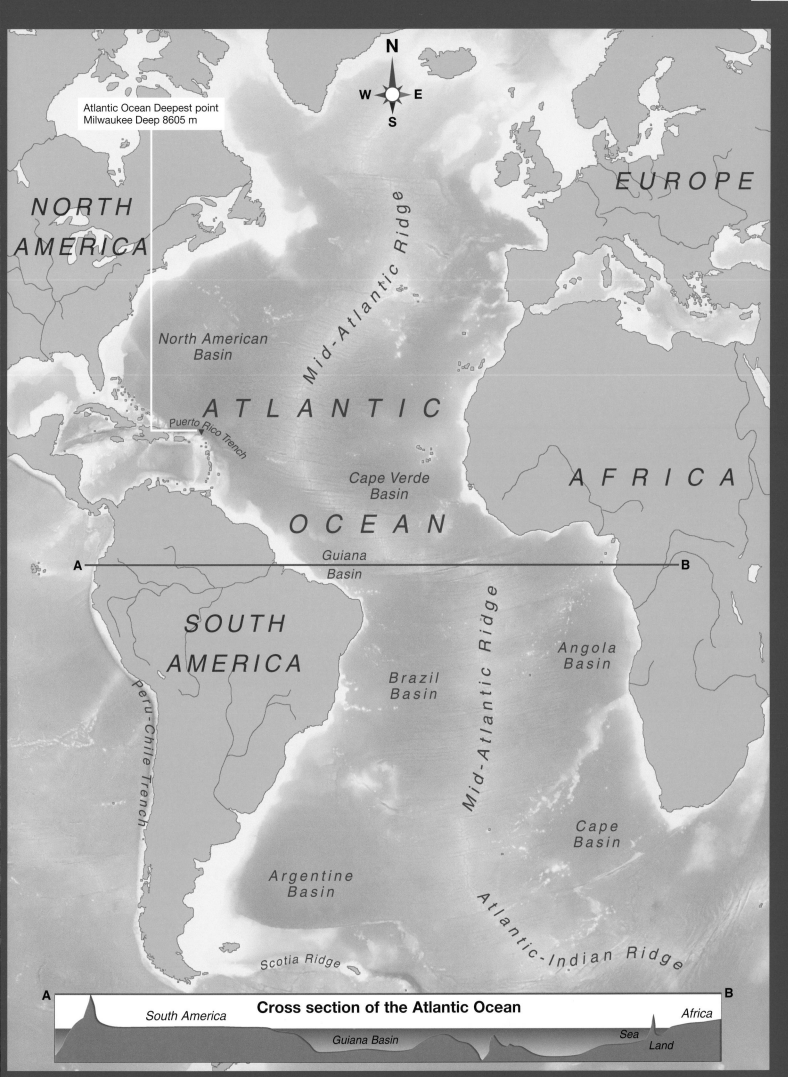

Atlantic Ocean Deepest point
Milwaukee Deep 8605 m

NORTH
AMERICA

EUROPE

North American
Basin

Mid-Atlantic Ridge

ATLANTIC

Puerto Rico Trench

Cape Verde
Basin

AFRICA

OCEAN

A

Guiana
Basin

B

SOUTH
AMERICA

Angola
Basin

Brazil
Basin

Mid-Atlantic Ridge

Peru-Chile Trench

Cape
Basin

Argentine
Basin

Atlantic-Indian Ridge

Scotia Ridge

A

Cross section of the Atlantic Ocean

B

South America

Africa

Guiana Basin

Sea

Land

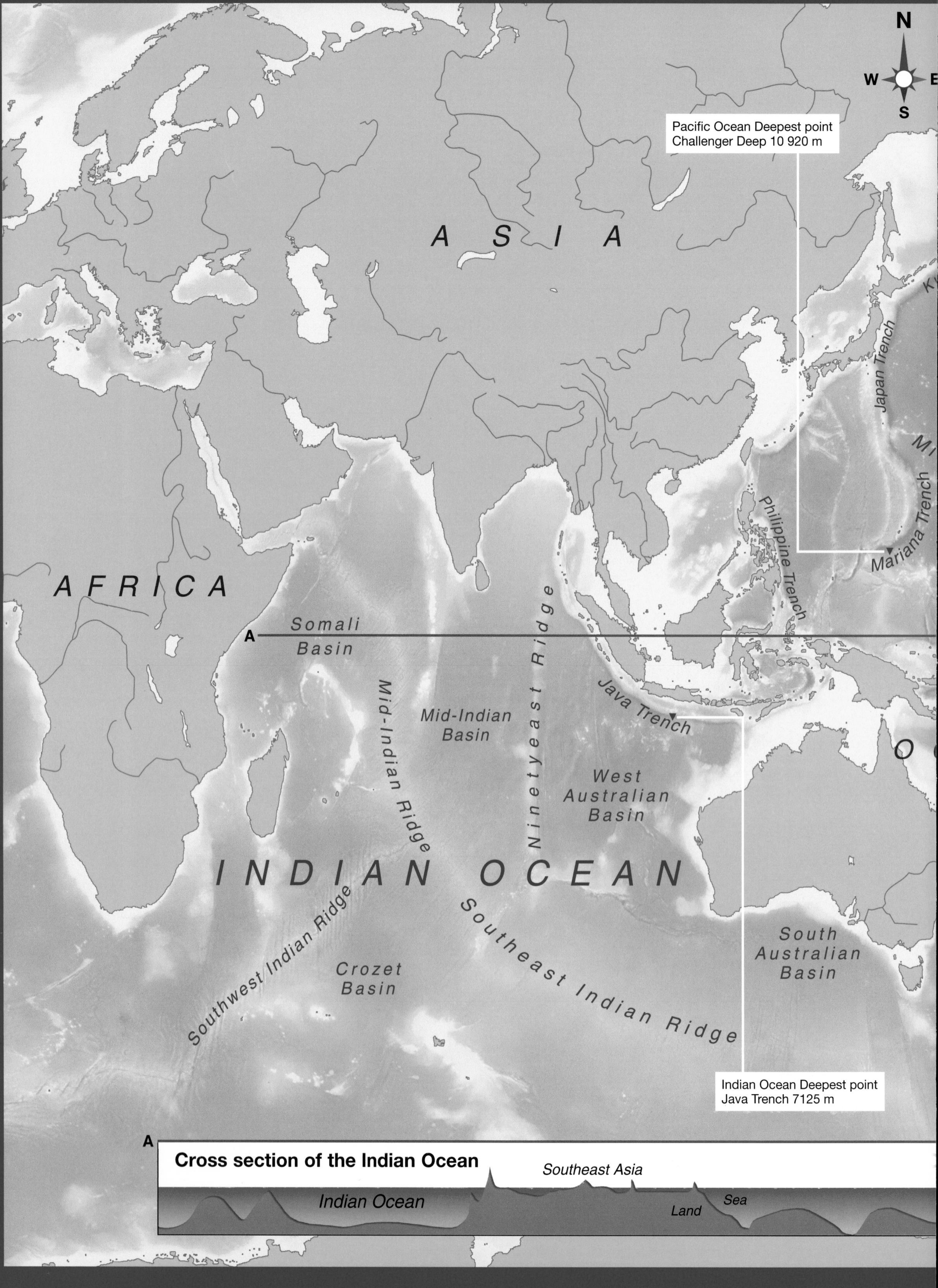

N
W E
S

Pacific Ocean Deepest point
Challenger Deep 10 920 m

A S I A

Japan Trench

Philippine Trench

Mariana Trench

A F R I C A

A *Somali
Basin*

Mid-Indian Ridge

*Mid-Indian
Basin*

Ninetyeast Ridge

Java Trench

*West
Australian
Basin*

I N D I A N   O C E A N

Southwest Indian Ridge

*Crozet
Basin*

Southeast Indian Ridge

*South
Australian
Basin*

Indian Ocean Deepest point
Java Trench 7125 m

A

Cross section of the Indian Ocean

Southeast Asia

Indian Ocean

Sea

Land

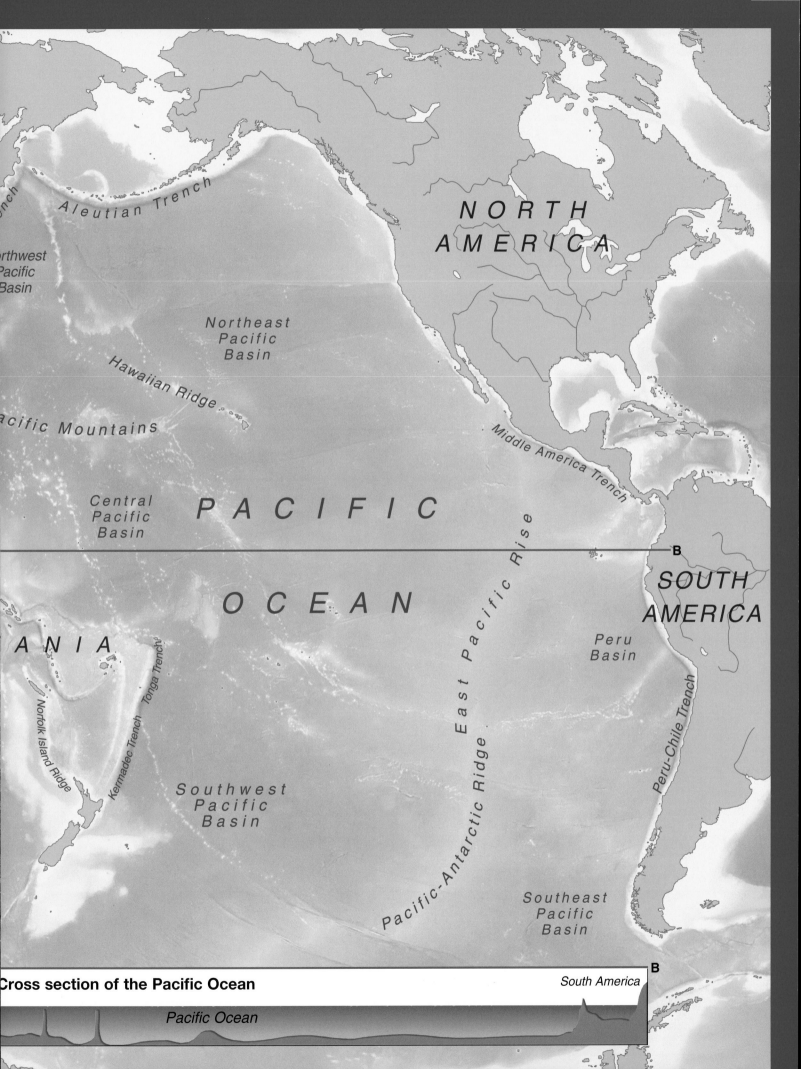

Aleutian Trench

Northwest Pacific Basin

NORTH AMERICA

Northeast Pacific Basin

Hawaiian Ridge

acific Mountains

Central Pacific Basin

PACIFIC

Middle America Trench

East Pacific Rise

B

SOUTH AMERICA

OCEAN

ANIA

Peru Basin

Norfolk Island Ridge

Kermadec Trench

Tonga Trench

Southwest Pacific Basin

Pacific-Antarctic Ridge

Peru-Chile Trench

Southeast Pacific Basin

B

Cross section of the Pacific Ocean

South America

Pacific Ocean

Key to symbols

- ～ River
- Lake
- Ice cap
- Polar pack ice
- Drifting ice

Land height above sea level in metres

over 2000 ....
1000 – 2000 ....
500 – 1000 ....
200 – 500 ....
0 – 200 ....

The British Isles at the same scale.

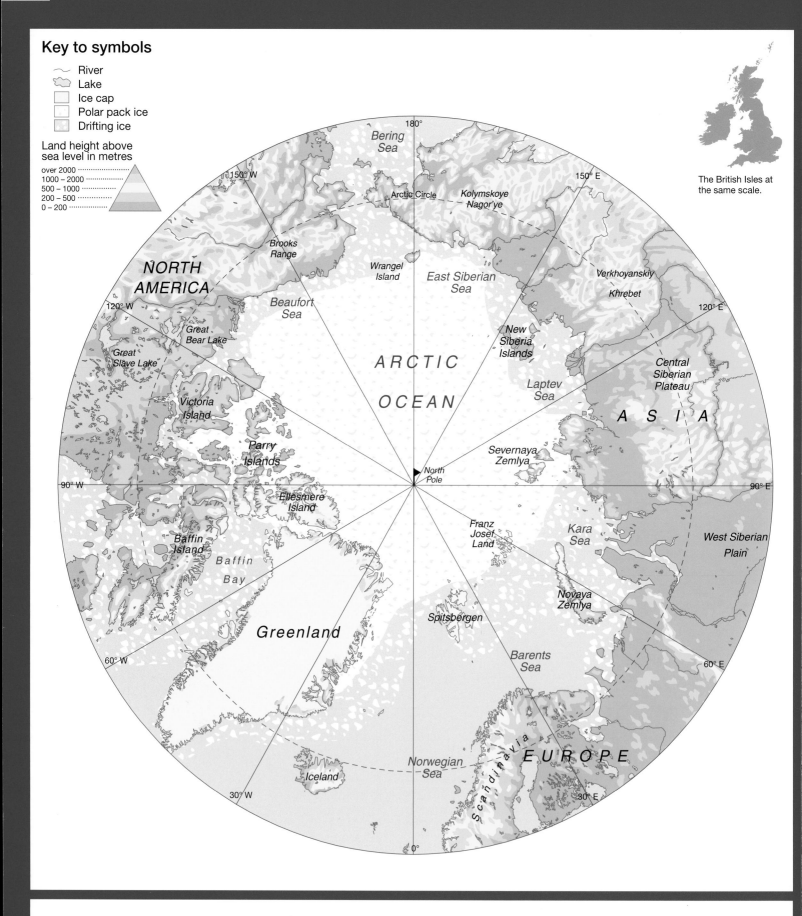

180°

Bering Sea

150° W

150° E

Arctic Circle

Kolymskoye Nagor'ye

Brooks Range

Wrangel Island

East Siberian Sea

Verkhoyanskiy Khrebet

120° E

NORTH AMERICA

Beaufort Sea

120° W

Great Bear Lake

New Siberia Islands

Central Siberian Plateau

Great Slave Lake

ARCTIC

A S I A

Victoria Island

OCEAN

Laptev Sea

Parry Islands

Severnaya Zemlya

North Pole

90° W

90° E

Ellesmere Island

Franz Josef Land

Kara Sea

Baffin Island

West Siberian Plain

Baffin Bay

Novaya Zemlya

Spitsbergen

Greenland

Barents Sea

60° W

60° E

Scandinavia

E U R O P E

Norwegian Sea

Iceland

30° W

30° E

0°

Cross section of the Arctic Ocean

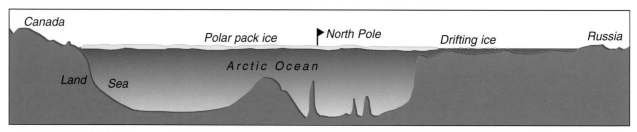

Canada

North Pole

Polar pack ice

Drifting ice

Russia

Land

Sea

Arctic Ocean

0   500   1000   1500   2000 km

Scale : One centimetre on this map is the same as 350 kilometres on the ground.

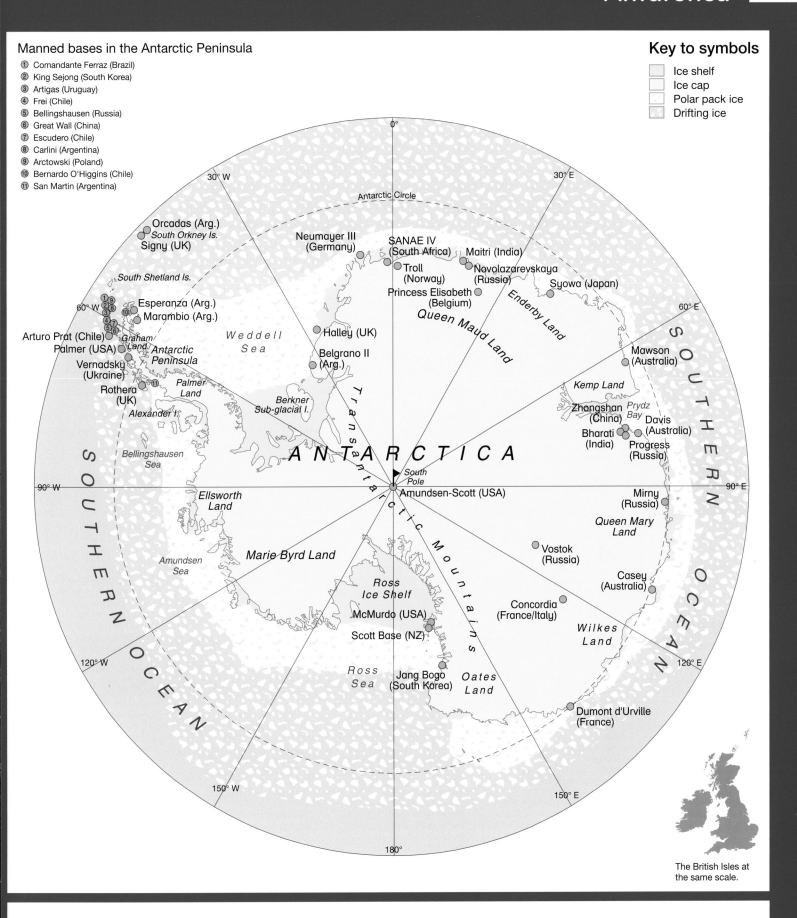

Manned bases in the Antarctic Peninsula
① Comandante Ferraz (Brazil)
② King Sejong (South Korea)
③ Artigas (Uruguay)
④ Frei (Chile)
⑤ Bellingshausen (Russia)
⑥ Great Wall (China)
⑦ Escudero (Chile)
⑧ Carlini (Argentina)
⑨ Arctowski (Poland)
⑩ Bernardo O'Higgins (Chile)
⑪ San Martin (Argentina)

Key to symbols
Ice shelf
Ice cap
Polar pack ice
Drifting ice

The British Isles at the same scale.

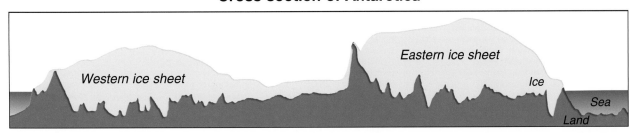

Cross section of Antarctica

Western ice sheet
Eastern ice sheet
Ice
Sea
Land

0 500 1000 1500 2000 km

Scale : One centimetre on this map is the same as 350 kilometres on the ground.

place name   grid code
Cairo *capital* 57 F5
page number
cities and towns are shown in green

place name   grid code
Tyne *river* 22 D4
page number
water features are shown in blue

place name   grid code
Italy *country* 28 G3
page number
countries and states are shown in red

place name   grid code
Corsica *island* 28 F3
page number
physical features are shown in black